# PIECES *of* ME

# PIECES *of* ME

## A Story of Hope and Restoration

### ESTHER JONES

XULON PRESS

Xulon Press
2301 Lucien Way #415
Maitland, FL 32751
407.339.4217
www.xulonpress.com

Due to the changing nature of the Internet, if there are any web addresses,
links, or URLs included in this manuscript, these may have been altered
and may no longer be accessible. The views and opinions shared in this
book belong solely to the author and do not necessarily reflect those of the
publisher. The publisher therefore disclaims responsibility for the views or
opinions expressed within the work.

Unless otherwise indicated, Scripture quotations taken from the Holy Bible,
New International Version (NIV). Copyright © 1973, 1978, 1984, 2011 by
Biblica, Inc.™. Used by permission. All rights reserved.

Scripture quotations taken from the King James Version (KJV) – *public domain.*

Paperback ISBN-13: 978-1-66282-779-2
Ebook ISBN-13: 978-1-66282-780-8

# TABLE OF CONTENTS

# ACKNOWLEDGMENTS

I want to thank these amazing peolple, who help edit my book for no charge, such a blessing. -Esther Jones

Cindy Carey
Micheal Mertinez
Becky Cacciatore

# INTRODUCTION

*This Is the story of the life of Esther Jones. The places she has gone been and what it took for her to get where she is today. And also why there is a great HOPE for her future. How all of her life's broken pieces from circumstances in her life fell into the right hands - God's hands. What brought her to suicide's door more than once. How she is now changed and set free from the curses of her past. How she learned what love truly is and how she learned to love the way she is meant to love. Although her journey is nowhere near done, she has come so far and grown so much in her very short life. This story is meant to show the struggle of her life in hopes to reach those who may be going through some of the same things she experienced - or even just to encourage you. No matter how big or small your problems are there is hope. God can help anyone, it doesn't matter who you are, what you may or may not have done, He is a loving God who has died so that we all may be SET FREE.*

# CHAPTER 1

# THE BEGINNING PIECES

*I*n the beginning I almost did not make it into this world at all. My mother questioned having me, her and my father's relationship was rocky from the start. Even before I was brought into this world there was already conflict and turmoil in their relationship. Unfortunately, I was not conceived by two people who had a healthy, happy relationship. My mother was still married in fact to my sister's and brother's father. I was conceived out of wedlock. For that reason, the joy that comes for parents in the thought of a new child, a new life wasn't there in the thought of me being born. More than anything else, there was worry, fear and doubt in my mother's mind unfortunately. Because of this, my mother had her mind made up to do the unthinkable… she was planning to have an abortion to erase the worry, fear and doubt she had in her mind. She made that appointment for me to be aborted. The appointment was set, would there be an Esther? Well as you know full well, I am here.

So, what happened, why and how did she change her mind? While she was at the appointment getting examined, she felt pain and she says she thinks I was curling up saying "no" being stubborn already! There is no way to confirm this - this was only something she says at the time she felt. I know it was God having his hand over my life even then because I know God has a plan for EVERY child conceived. So, as she felt this pain she got up and called my grandmother and asked her mom "what should I do, I don't know if I should do this." My grandmother then said, "if you don't feel in your heart to do this, don't do it." (My grandmother wasn't happy about this pregnancy) After having this conversation with my grandmother, even though my mother had been prepped and ready to go through with it, she searched her heart and said NO, and got up and left! So, *there* was a beginning for me.

I was born Oct 3, 1987, in Brooklyn, NY - the Big Apple as they call it. I was brought to my grandmother's house on 11th street in Brooklyn. My mother left my sister's and brother's father moving back in temporarily with my grandmother until she then decided to move and start a life with my father. We lived in a few different places on this street but no matter how many times we moved; grandma's house was always the one consistent place we called home. I spent a lot of time there. There were many good memories, as well as not so good memories made in this place I called "home."

From as young as I can remember in this place was a place full of many ups and downs. I remember always feeling unwanted here, although it was a place to call "home" it was also the place where rejection entered my life.

My grandmother as I stated earlier was not happy. Regarding my birth, she was not happy with many of my mother's choices at the time. The choice of my father for one she never liked him, therefore the thought of me and my birth was not the happiest of thoughts. But she loved and wanted to support my mother. Her being her daughter, so it was as if my grandmother grew to have a love yet underlying hate and resentment of me. From the moment I was born I had a lot and still do have a lot of my father's features as well as my mom's but there was no denying I was my father's child. I wasn't always treated the best by my grandmother. She provided for me, made sure I had food and was physically cared for but always had this underlying hate for me. It seemed no matter what I did throughout the years I was never good enough. As my story goes on those pieces will slowly be revealed of how she also brought so much rejection and took out lots of her anger out on me throughout my life. Using physical and emotional abuse every chance she got all because of the hatred in her heart for my father, because I was a part of him. This for me seemed to be a trend in my family being unwanted the "annoying kid". I was the youngest of all the children in my family. My brother being 10 years older than me and my sister being 7 years. I always remember many times where I felt alone. As I have a brother and sister, who would play with me from time to time, but as time went on and the age gap seemed to get bigger them getting older. In the mist of so much chaos at times there where some good memories the early years from 4 to 8 years old were some good times, happy memories and moments. This being before my mother and father's drug use began to destroy any hope for a great family and childhood. Although even in these years my childhood and family were far from not being chaotic and unhealthy. Now looking back now and understanding it as I do now as an adult. My family has always been dysfunctional. There has never been a time where there was not yelling and screaming. Yet at least there were happy moments within them. The first that comes to mind is when I learned to ride a bike, my father helped. I remember him letting go and the feeling of "yes I can do it!" then realizing I did not know how to stop! Holidays with the family all together at grandma's house (moms' side of the family) My aunt Cookie one of my favorite aunts, had three children Steven, Michael and Janine were also older than me with large gaps in age, like my brother and sister. She was married to my uncle Vido, he was always super quiet, but very funny. He was always telling jokes making me laugh. My mother also had a brother his kids Alexis and Karimah as well as his then wife Barbara one of my other favorites and last but not least my mother also had a sister Dee Dee who a couple years after I was born passed away, but I still had her two children in my life David and Susan. So, this was most of family that came around during the happy holidays at grandma's house. My maternal grandfather father was also around, he and my grandmother divorced years before I was even born. I again was the youngest like 7 or more years younger. One of my favorite memeries with my grandmother was the time we danced to "Grandma Got Run Over by a Reindeer" as we put up Christmas lights. Times walking to school with my mom during winter and throwing snow -also her falling on ice and us laughing so hard as she sat on the ground! Playing cards with my sister (Uno), I always lost! Running home from school with my brother. I remember feeling like I was flying because we were going so fast! One time we were running home, I fell because we were going so fast and downhill nonetheless! I still have the scar to this day to remind me, Halloweens getting dressed up and trick or treating with both my parents and siblings, we even did family bike rides to prospect park in Brooklyn. I remember my dad was always the star dad of the park because he would always be the big kid playing with me and other kids. Also doing tricks on the monkey bars. There were a lot of weekends spent with my father's side of the family as well, where I had MANY cousins to play with. My father had many sisters and brothers I'll just name a few my aunt Zola who was I just remember being so sweet, my aunt Jenny who was silly and fun, aunt Charlene who was the crazy, silly and the most outgoing of them all, and there's my favorite uncle Nikki that super cool fun uncle. Cannot forget my sweet aunt Robin. There were many family gatherings, BBQs, and sleep overs with my father's side of the family. So many cousins to play with. That was the best part my father's side of the family I was not the youngest. I had cousins of all ages it was always a fun adventure when I got to see them all. I was though my father's only child, he was the only sibling with one child. One of the things I would often do with my father that I thought was just the best was going to the store to buy CANDY! That made any day better! These years I wish lasted because although there was bad the good times at least were good. It seemed like time went on, life just began to become hugely different. In these good years there still was a lot of dysfunctions our family wasn't ever "the happy family" but at least there was some happy moments in these early years. Also some of these memories that aren't so good would and did scar me for a very long time. At five years old I was traumatized by my father to be in fear of Chucky (the killer horror doll from the movies) as well as the Freddy Kruger character. First with Chucky, one day after work my father brought me home a doll in a paper bag with only the feet sticking out and gave it to me. At this point, I was already afraid of Chucky being that I had seen some of the movies. When my father handed me bag with the doll, I was at first so excited that my daddy brought me a new toy! When I opened it and realized it was Chucky, I flung it against the wall! My father then got really upset, grabbing me by the ponytail put me up against the wall yelling in my face saying "what the f^&%$ are you afraid of its Just a doll, no kid of mine is gonna be afraid of no doll! There's nothing to be afraid of, you're gonna sleep with this in your room!" That night I remember staying up, staring at the doll until I heard silence though the house - I then got up and threw the doll out of the room! Finally, I was able to get to sleep. The next thing I remember is waking up to a doll on my STOMACH talking! I began shaking as if I was having a seizure and then my father turned on the lights, laughing saying "its ok Its only me!" I remember this so clearly. Fear became a part of my life at an incredibly young age, it is something I battled with for many years. I can think back and always remember being afraid of one thing or another. One of the biggest things I remember is being afraid of looking under my bed, walking into a dark room or even opening a closet. I was told things like, "watch out Chuckey's in there!" and the laughter that followed. These things started with my father, and he eventually thought and made the whole family do to me thinking it was funny. What they thought was so "funny" did more damage and harm and would affect my life, greater than they would ever know or imagine. Many people reading this now, may be thinking "Well, that's just normal. That's just what families do." For many years I thought it was normal myself, and that I was silly for being so afraid of something so fake and obviously not real, right? Wrong. I thought this way for years, that it something was wrong with me for feeling this way. I felt I was the silly, crazy one for being so afraid. Well, you will find out later in my story that as my life went on, this so-called "silly joke" continued to affect me. So no, if you think these things are normal let me be the first to say they are not because this fear became a part of me, like another limb on my body that was always there. Not to mention the countless times where my parents physically fight. It would go from arguing to yelling louder and louder to things being thrown and then eventually a fight breaking out. Even with the happy memories there was always dysfunction. Although these years were not the worst years, I would not say the best ether. They may have been the best years of my childhood because there was function in the mist of so much dysfunction. But soon the drug use began to take over. I started to become more aware of how dysfunctional things were and had become the more and I had been exposed things and My life slowly but surely would take a turn for worse, as drug use and anger took over my parents lives little by little and so did my life begin to change little by little.

CHAPTER 2

# HAPPY PIECES BECOME BROKEN PIECES

ow did happy pieces turn into broken pieces? A memory is what good times had become because life as I knew it began to change slowly then quickly and drastically at the same time it seemed. The good times seemed to fade away as life continued. Unfortunately, the bad began to outweigh the good.

As time went on drugs became a bigger problem for both of my parents. This is where everything really started to fall apart. I knew and understood what drugs were and when they were being used. Things began to get progressively worse. Soon keeping up with a family of five, paying bills and supporting their drug habit became overwhelming for both my parents. As the financial pressure and drug use grew, my parents would fight daily. It would escalate from verbal to physical very quickly.

Unfortunately, us kids got caught in the crossfire. I remember many times hiding, covering my ears, crying, and waiting for it to be over. I was so young, so scared. With no security and not knowing when these fights would start again. As time went on, things just went from bad to worse. I wanted to run, but how and where? Besides, this was my "mommy and daddy", I could not ever imagine life without them. I was devoted to them no matter what happened. At an incredibly young age, my brother left. He and my father did not get along at the time because my brother wanted to protect my mom from their physical fights. This would lead to my brother and father physically fighting. The fights just seemed to get worse and soon my mother and father separated. Soon after they separated, my mother made a life-changing decision to move to a new home without telling my dad. She wanted to create a new life, a new fresh start. Our move from New York to Florida would be the best for all of us, she said. Soon after making up her mind on this new life, she and my brother left to Florida, leaving me and my sister with my grandmother. Until we finished school. Living with my grandmother was not easy for me. I believe she had an underline hated for me because of the way my father treated my mother. My grandmother took out on me all of her anger and resentment toward me because I was a part of him. I was always treated differently from the rest of her grandkids. She was very hard on me. She had a small room in her house, when I would visit or stay for any amount of time. She would put me in there for hours, sometimes even whole days. If she felt I had disrespected her or just simply annoyed her in any way. I would have to ask to come out to go to the bathroom, eat or drink anything.

I remember thinking "what can I do to make her love me? why did she hate me?"

My father found out my mother's plan and followed her to Florida, proclaiming his love for her and she took him back. I was eight years old when my sister and I arrived in Florida that summer. I remember thinking how different this new place was and feeling hope for our family's new future there. Things changed for a while, but eventually things got back to the way they were with my parents. The drugs never stopped, the addiction was there and just got stronger. The physical abuse between my parents began again. One day I remember they were fighting in the living room, and I was in another room and hearing what was going on. After hearing what sounded like a tornado going through the house as things were being thrown around, I walked into the room, and it looked like a war zone. My parents were going at each other back and forth my mother was so angry. She threw a lamp across the room that lamp hit my father right in the head. It hit him just in the right area of his head the next thing I knew my father's head was gushing blood everywhere. On to the walls, ceiling, and floor, it was everywhere. It looked like murder scene right in our living room. My mother went from angry and screaming to just down right scared. Going to my father's aid helping him holding a rag on his head saying, "awe man look at what the F@#$& you made me do!" I was so afraid, crying in the corner of the room. A neighbor had called the cops because they heard them fighting. It went very quickly from a moment of watching my mom help my father holding a rag to his head, to the police knocking on the door. It was crazy I remember it was like a switch with both of my parents. They went from being so angry and yelling at each other to showing compassion and love to one another in front of the cops saying that it was just an argument, an accident. I remember so clearly the cops pushing my father, wanting him to get my mom in trouble pressing charges against her for his head. Then seeing him refuse and saying, "It's all good it was an accident". He was taken to the hospital because he had to get stitches in his head.

This was just one example of many times this occurred. More and more, the good times were fading away and the bad really began to overshadow everything else. By this point, when good things happened, I always expected that it wouldn't last long. I never could appreciate good times because they seemed to come and go like the wind. Things stayed this way for quite a while. This is what life was like this became normalcy for us. I always longed to know what other family-life was like what real normal family was. About a year after creating this life in Florida, nothing got better and we moved to a different place. Things continued to remain the same. From bad to terrible - the situation got worse after about a year of being in this new home. At this point, my mom had experienced things in her relationship with my father that she could never have imagined. She said, "enough was enough", her and my father finally separated again. This left me feeling so much hurt and confusion. I knew the things that went on were not acceptable or normal, but he was my daddy and she was mommy and they were supposed to be together.

CHAPTER 3

# PIECES OF CONFUSION
# AND LONELINESS

With my father out of the picture, now it's just my mother, myself and my sister. My brother moved back to New York to be with his girlfriend at the time (she later became his wife). My heart was completely broken at age 10. My daddy was gone, life was still unhealthy. I yearned for love, real love, untainted love. I was still devoted to my parents and still had this hope inside that things would get better. This is when confusion and loneliness set in for me. My mother soon had to figure out how to be a single mother after being with my father for 18 years. This is when my mother fell into a deep, deep depression due to all her pain, guilt, and shame of not knowing how to move forward. The mother who once had help with parenting to now trying to do everything. She didn't know how to cope with that, so she fell deeper into drugs to cover up her hurt. This affected me because I was so young and had to grow up so fast. My sister was still at home with me, but she fell into her own hurt and found her own way to cope. It seemed as though during this time my mother was never home and when she was, it wasn't ever left pleasant - yelling and screaming constantly most of the time for almost no reason. The times she was gone, she left me with my sister who is 7 years older. She was dealing with her own hurts and ways of dealing with it. Not really having her mother around much anymore having no guidance. Being a rebellious teen. Leaving me alone to fend for myself.

Living at the same place where my father first left, I had a few friends not many. One friend was a boy "Jimmy," we played all the time. His family situation was a little different as both his parents were deaf, but Jimmy had his hearing. We had many memorys and aventures. One that sticks out the most is , I remember dreaming of the day I would be married, as most young girls do. I came up with this idea of a fake wedding, complete with flowers and a dress I found. He and I would go from playing house and other girly things to rollerblading and flying off ramps we created and built. There was also an older girl Rachel who I hung out with from time to time. She was a few years older than me. Christmas day that year, my mom asked Rachels mom if I could stay there. Because somehow our family dinner burnt in the oven. My mother had to go to the grocery store. Her Rachels mother said it was ok. It did not go so well for me; they had a vicious dog who was only friendly to them. Every time I saw this dog outside barking and growling. On this day, the girl said "well, you're in my house, she will probably be nice to you." She showed me how she would give the dog a treat and after it would lick her face. Then she said to me, "here's a treat, why don't you try it" so I did it, after seeing the dog do it with her. The dog did lick me face but as I pulled away, it then bit my face! I remember going into the bathroom to look at my face and seeing nothing but blood. She then called her mom and her mom rushed to my house with a bag of ice over my face. I was rushed to the emergency room. Because of the bag and towel on my face the whole time in the middle of the rushing around, my mom never saw my face to see how bad the damage really was. When we arrived at the emergency room, they told us to have a seat and that's when my mom took the bag off my face. She now could see skin hanging and started to lose it. The emergency room nurses then took me back right away and had to give me plastic surgery to fix what the dog had done. After this incident I was not able to play over her house anymore.

At this time of my life with everything that was going on at home, it was good to have friends to escape it all. But soon after my dad leaving, we moved and from that point on it seemed like friends were nothing but a memory. I had no friends at the new place we moved to. More than ever, I remember longing for a friend. I was left home alone so often, and loneliness seemed to be my only friend, not a good one. School though, school was my only escape. Most kids disliked school, but no, not me. I loved it. Being around others without all the craziness going on around me was something I looked forward to. I had many sweet teachers who I grew close to. My mother warned me never to tell anyone at school about the things I knew were going on at home, if did I would be taken away from my family.

Logically speaking, Some may think that would have been the best thing for me. But I loved my mother so much, it did not matter what the situation was at home, I could not imagine life without her. No matter what may or may not have happened in my life. I always had hope things would get better. "We will be happy someday" I would tell myself. Because of this love for her, I knew to never talk about home and when I was asked, I knew just what to say.

Out of all teachers that touched my life there was one that stuck out more than the rest, Mrs. Johnson. She knew something was going on at home but never seemed to ask too many questions. She just took me under her wing. I was the teacher's pet in our 5th grade class. Some of the other students did not like that she treated me so well. After her showing just a little love and attention that I always longed for, I began to cling to her. I would do all I could to stay after school and help her in the classroom. For me, anything was better than being home. Even if it was helping to clean - it did not matter. I would want to sit with her in class and draw pictures all the time instead of doing my classwork. It was a love I had never known. As the year went on, we got closer. She would bring me home many times after school. Then one day, after always talking to my mom on the phone, she finally met with my mother face to face as she was dropping me off. She complimented me, telling my mother how much help I was to her. Mrs. Johnson also asked permission to take me out one Saturday afternoon. My mom then asked me to walk the dog as they continued to talk. When I got back, Mrs. Johnson was gone. My mother told me she agreed for her to take me out next Saturday and told me it was a surprise and that she could not tell me what we were doing or where we were going. I remember being so excited, more than I had ever been in a long time. The next day at school I tried to talk to her about it, and she would not tell me anything. She then asked for me not talk about it at school. The day was finally here and I anxiously waited for her to arrive. My mother waited outside for her and soon after came in to let me know Mrs. Johnson was outside. I ran to the door so excited, said goodbye to my mother, and ran down the stairs to Mrs. Johnson's car. I got in and asked her "ok, where are we going, you can tell me now right?" She then said nope, it's still a surprise, so I waited. This was such a great memory; I remember the exact song I heard on the radio - "Maria Maria" by Carlos Santana. We then got to where we were going, it was her daughter's hockey game. Her daughter was about 5 years older than me, and the surprise was to bring me out to one of her games. After the game, the three of us went back to her house to have dinner. I remember this was the first time I had ever seen a family without chaos. For the first time, I saw a family together with no screaming, yelling and all the negative things I was used to seeing. I felt as though I was in a dream. I was so upset at the thought of leaving and going home, I wanted to stay in this place forever. It was that day I saw for the first time what a normal functional family was, that day at 10 years old I made my mind up that someday I wanted to be like they were and not the way my family was. I went home that night with a smile on my face, yet sad that the night was over. The school year went on and things stayed the same - me staying after school, her driving me home. She would often stop for a bit and talk to my mom. Then it was Christmas time. Christmas time was not always all that exciting at this time in my life because we were far from the family, and we knew (me and my sister) that my mom didn't have much money. She would tell us, "Well, you're not getting much this year."

This Christmas for me was different, a Christmas I will never forget!

Mrs. Johnson sent home a letter I was told not to open but let us just say I was a very curious and nosy child. I did in fact open the letter and read that she would be getting me Christmas gifts. When she was bringing them that I was unsure of when she would bring them.

Then one night after school, Mrs. Johnson brought me home and came inside to talk to my mom. Mrs. Johnson, she needed to talk to my mother alone asked me to go to my room. My mother asked me instead to go walk the dog, I did. I just knew she was up to something. When I came back inside, Mrs. Johnson was gone, I asked "my mom what's going on? am I going somewhere?" My mom said "nothing, "I'm not telling you nothing" she said. One night while she was gone, I went on a search in my mother's room hoping that she had gotten me something for Christmas. Then there I saw it, a big Macy's bag. As I pushed down on the bag to see what was inside, there was air in the bag. The air shot up to my face and it smelled like Mrs. Johnson, and I knew she had brought these gifts for me. I did not see any gifts, just the boxes. They were all in gift boxes of all sizes. Then my sister walked into the room saying, "what are you doin?" I jumped and began closing the bag and she said "I'm telling. You were not supposed to be in there!" I finished closing the bag and ran out of the room. Then later it got worse when my mom came home that night. She yelled and screamed and carried on saying "What the F**** were you doing in there, huh? Why were you in my closet, you had no business in there." I then said "I know. I'm sorry. I didn't see what was in the boxes." I was sent to my room for the rest of the night. It was Christmas break; my grandfather came down for the week. For Christmas he bought me a new bike and told me this was, so I didn't have to be taken to school. I could ride my bike. Finally, it was Christmas morning. I woke up to a tree full of presents with my name all over them. It was the best Christmas in a long time. I remember feeling so excited as I opened each gift. There were board games, clothes, and Barbies, all my favorite things.

Over the school break, I talked to Mrs. Johnson once or twice over the phone. She then asked if she could take me to church with her that Sunday and my mom agreed. I had been to church growing up, a Pentecostal Christian church, but this was the first time I had ever gone to a Catholic church. I remember it being so quiet and peaceful. It was back to school on Monday. The rest of the year remained the same between her and me. I remember becoming saddened as the year progressed, knowing that it would all end soon, as everything else did in my life. I did not want it to end, it just could not. I wanted to stay in this place in my life forever. Up until this point, with all that I had gone through, it was a happy piece I did not want to lose. I had this attachment to her, a love it seemed I had waited my whole life. As the year ended, Mrs. Johnson told me that we would see one another. Within a week of school ending, she told me she was moving to another Elementary school, and I could come and visit her whenever I wanted, even though it was a different school. Now, as the school year ended, it was not so bad knowing I would not lose her.

As the Summer went on, the calls stopped, and I had not seen her all summer. I was so upset thinking "What have I done? Surely I must have done something." I also began thinking, as she told me she loved me, that she did not anymore. This completely tore me apart. I did not know where she lived to send her a letter so I just dealt with it all summer long. Beating up myself, thinking I must have done or said something, that it was somehow all my fault.

The next school year began, and I moved on to 6th grade at a new school. Then after about a week or two, I ran into another student that had a younger sibling at the school were Mrs. Johnson was teaching. She said they had seen her and that she took care of the younger kids after school there. This news made me extremely excited and because I knew where the school was. It was within bike-riding distance from where we lived. Right away I came up with this plan to get in touch with her again. I did two things - I went to the school the next afternoon and not only did I go there, but I also wrote her a letter just in case she was not there for some reason. Good thing I did because she was not there. I saw the janitor and gave him the letter and he said he had put it in her mailbox for me. He then told me the days she was there after school so next time I would come on the right day.

The day came and on my way there I was so happy, yet nervous thinking it may be my fault that she stopped all contact. I saw the janitor and he directed me to where she was and what classroom to go to. As I got closer to her classroom, I can remember hearing her voice after not hearing it for so long. I put my back up the against the wall and began crying, second guessing if I should go in. I figured since I came all this way, I must go in, so I did. I could not just walk in, I had to do it in a silly way of course. I crawled on the floor hoping to really surprise her. When I was halfway in, one of her students yelled "Mrs. Johnson, there is someone crawling on the floor, and I don't know who it is!" I then popped up and she saw it was me she ran to me embracing me with a hug and said "Don't you ever say I do not love you; I do and always will, I got your letter". She then sat me down and began to tell me why she lost touch. I hung out for a little while then it was time for me to leave. She told me not to worry, that I could come and visit her anytime I wanted at this new school. After that, every week at least once a week, I would go and visit her. Then one night after getting home from visiting her, my mom said she had to tell me something. I only visited with Mrs. Johnson at this point for about 2 or 3 weeks and then my mom told me the news that we were moving back to New York in two weeks! With my mother's addiction, we never stayed anywhere for too long. This news completely tore me apart and I immediately began to cry. My mom then asked me "What you are crying for?!" I then told her it was because I did not want to leave Mrs. Johnson. She then really lost it saying things like "She doesn't do anything for you, I do! What the F**** do you need her for!" and so much more. After this, I do not remember much but yelling. I then remember going to my room holding my school picture, looking at Mrs. Johnson crying, thinking that I just could not bear to lose her, not again. I cried myself to sleep that night and the next week.

I went to see Mrs. Johnson and I was so upset when I got there that she came to me right away wondering what was wrong. I told her the news and began crying even more as the truth of why I was upset came out. She embraced me, telling me that everything would be ok and that we would write each other and talk on the phone. At this moment, after this sadness the anger set in. I felt the one thing that brought happiness to my life, the love that I had always longed for was being taken from me! I then said to her "NO I'M GONNA RUN AWAY!" I couldn't bear the thought of losing her. She grabbed my shoulders, bent down and looked me in the eyes and said "Esther, you are not gonna do that, your gonna go home and stay with your mom, promise me Esther, promise me!" I looked at her and said " Ok, I promise but I just don't want to lose you." She hugged me and we sat together for a while. Then it was time for me to go and she said, "ok Esther its time". I cried, " I don't want to go." She took off her sweater and said here, keep this, it is cold anyway. Take this and every-time is you miss me, put this on, close your eyes and I will be there with you giving you a hug. I left in tears. I cried all the way home on my bike, with the tears running down my face feeling like icicles.

(Writing this now the memory brings me right back to the same feelings. From that night the devastation that I felt as a little girl. Bringing me right back to those moments) I got home again, crying myself to sleep as I now slept with the sweater she had given me.

That next week we did move to New York. We went, my sister stayed behind, and she moved in with her boyfriend. My mom and I, for the first couple of months lived with my grandmother.

I was enrolled in middle school, MS 88 in Brooklyn where my grandmother lived. A few months after living with my grandmother, we moved to our own apartment in Bed-Stuy (Bedford/Stuyvesant), Brooklyn. I had to be enrolled in a school with my grandmother's address because Bed-Stuy at the time was not a good neighborhood, I'm not sure how it is now. I had to ride two trains at 12 years old (soon going on 13), by myself every day to get to school because my maternal grandmother lived about 30 minutes away from where we were in Bed-Stuy. This was scary for me but at times it got *really* scary. Two times that stick out in my memory. Once, they had to stop the train because there were two gangs running after each other with knives. They ran right passed me, running off the train. They made it to the car I was in because they were hopping the cars, going from car to car after each other.

I honestly believe that God protected through the next thing that happened. I got off one train at a stop and I was waiting for the next train. It was really quiet. I thought I was the only one waiting I looked around to see if I was right. As I looked to my left there was an incredibly quiet man staring at me, it was just me and him. He looked kind of rough. After I then noticed he was moving one of his arms I then looked down to see what he was doing and that is when I noticed his pants were bulged out and the area he was rubbing. He wasn't close to me, but he also wasn't very far. After I noticed what he was doing I imagine I must have made a face and he smiled at me. That creepy "I'm gonna get you" kind of smile. He then started walking toward me. I was frozen for a moment thinking this is not really happening. I started walking toward he exit, and he still followed.

Just then as I was getting ready to turn the corner out the exit, with him still behind, a woman police officer came around the corner. I remember the feeling of relief. She was also going on the train, so I turned around and as I did, I saw him walking away back in the direction he came from. Then the train came, and I went on the same cart as the officer and felt safe. I do not know what could or would have happened had that officer not shown up at the moment she did. I believe that it was God's protection. Living in this new home in bed-stye I was able make friends again there were a lot of kids on the block where I lived. The song " Festia" that was popular at the time and everyone I knew on the block would say "Ayyy what up festia" one time (as we all use to do with music) one of my friends played the song as I was walking home. He planned it so that when he saw me it would be playing.

People on the block all would stick speakers out the windows and play music. It was ok, until people started battling to see whose music was the loudest.

Now you must be thinking confusion and loneliness all these people around you how is this possible?

Well, it was very much so because I was never really close with anyone. No doubt there where people around, but not my family, not loved ones. They were all hurt and broken kids with their own issues going on at home. At this time of my life my mother's drug use was at an all-time high. School once again became my escape. This was where I was always reminded that I was in fact a kid. For the first time that I can ever remember in my life, I had a group of girl friends in this new middle school. We called our self's the CCCC's. I was "Coconut" there was

"Caramel" "Chocolate" and a few others I don't remember all names starting with "C". All us girls it was nice for the time it lasted my fun escape. I still remember feeling alone although I finally had fun close girlfriends. Because when you are the only one in your world that knows the hurt and secrets you harbor its defiantly a very lonely place. It is a whole part of life that you cannot share even with your closest friend. For two reasons: you are trained not to, also it is not the most popular thing to share. You want your friends to know how good your life and family is not how bad it is. All us girls where close but Cee Cee she was the closest to me. We spent a lot of time together. We had many sleepovers at hers and my house. I remember all my friends thought it was the coolest thing to stay over my house with my mother being out most of the time we pretty much did what we wanted. I have to say though now thinking of it having such freedom. We were pretty responsible I mean we didn't really do anything that I can remember being too bad. Other than staying up late and blasting music late at night. Oh, and the best was us climbing in and out of my bedroom window. The stairs to the building where right outside my window making it easy to go in and out on to the stairs beside the window. We didn't sneak out either we just went in and out that way because we could. Along with Cee Cee another girl Jay would also over who was also a part of our girl group. I remember them just loving it at my house and saying how funny my mother was. They had no clue just what life was really like for me. I also would from time to time stay over at Cee Cee's house and boy that a different world. So many siblings so, so much fun! Cee Cee's mom was always super sweet to me. She would go from talking sweet to me to the next second and yelling disciplining her own children for one reason or another. There were these small momentary escapes for me like this where I was just a kid. But within these moments it also would not make the loneliness I feel any better. I became as I did with many other kids became jealous of their lives. All that they had. I also began to grow tired of pretending that life was something it clearly was not.

# CHAPTER 4

# PIECES OF ABANDONMENT

My father also popped into my life for a short month or so before he was caught by the police for something he had done in Florida then fled to New York to escape. Before he was caught my mother allowed him to come and see me, this was a Happy time with him. It was short lived but none-theless a happy time. At this point I had not seen him for three years. With both my parents there was always this hope. he thought this time will be different. I had hope for a new begin-ning and a new start with them believing things would just be different. The sad truth is happy and good change where like a blink of an eye for me, the times came and then went just like that. Having him around this time was fun it almost as if all the physical and mental abuse that happened just three years prior never happened. When he was fun, he was just so much fun. He was always such a big kid he was that crazy dad playing with me and the rest of the kids outside. From hopscotch, double dutch and basketball you name it he played it with all of us. All my friends just loved him the girls Cee Cee and Jay even got to meet him when he came to visit. This was also three years after he and my mother broke up. With that ending so badly my mother now had fallen into drug use worse than she had ever father than he had even seen her. He had no idea how bad things had been at the time for me. Until one night I told him, and he was so upset at the thought of me having to care for myself at 12. For days at a time that one night when he had visited me, she had been gone for a day or so he asked, "will she be back tonight?" I told him that I had no clue but was scared asked if he could stay over or stay till, she came home. He did. I remember him telling me "Don't worry about it baby I'm here. Go to sleep" As I closed my eyes, he slept next to me on the floor. A few hours later in the middle of the night I was woken up by hearing my mother come home screaming telling him "get out asking why he was still there?" Then I listened to them argue as I had so many times before. Shortly after I did, not see him come around much more and my mother told me he was put in jail. Of course, there I was again happiness ripped away. As for my mother there things just counited to worsen, the drugs became even more important than me more than they ever had before. It was the beginning the, the beginning for a 12-year-old girl that was already so lost and broken. The start of the one of the worse years of my life. No matter what the circumstance I was still her protector, if I would ever get questioned by the other parents or teachers anyone who would ask. Asking things like "where she was?" If they had not seen her or "how she was doing?" I always knew just what to say, again she was still my mommy whom I loved and had to protect no matter what, right?!? Well soon after some even more hurtful things began to happen, I started to let my guard down thinking I need help. What were these things? or thing that would bring me to a point of exposing of my "mommy" in a moment of weakness?

It was a bad time in my mother, I was to endure it to go through it with no option or choice because she made the choice for me by fallen deeper into her drug use, she took me with her. I was only 13 I thought, I knew what loneliness was, but I soon realized that until this point, I had not known loneliness like this. I thought I had no idea how bad things were going to get. what the feeling of Abandonment was until this point. She began leaving me for days at a time to fed for myself. To feed, cloth, do everything for myself fully as an adult would have to. The "mommy" that I knew the love that I had somewhat even in a small way my whole life was now GONE this time. For the next year of my life adult hood as I knew it would have to fully be mine. (If not "they" would find out). "They" meaning the state child services. From a young age it was installed in me. I had grown to protect her no one knew how bad things were. When she would come home, I barely spoke to her and when I did it was not pleasant. She would almost never come home alone; she had her many drug friends that could care less about me. I would at times cry myself to sleep because, fear as I knew it would eat me up inside speak to me more at this time of my life. but not just that I just got downright tired I wanted a mommy I wanted to know what it was like to be normal, to have someone around who cared. Many of my friend's moms on the block where not home a-lot but it was because they worked a-lot and hard. At least these kids had that reassurance that their mom was coming and would come home. Of course, there lives were not perfect, nowhere near as bad as my situation. Sometimes my mother's friends or neighbors would ask where my mother was? If they had not seen her in a while.

I knew just what to say, so many different things like "oh she's sleeping", or "she went to the store shell be back" I will tell her u said "hello". (Writing this now it brings me back, back that little girl and how I felt. Tears fill my eyes thinking of how much the abandonment hurt and how so much I wanted things to be different. Wanted her at times just to hold me and love me to tell me everything's gonna be ok.) This desire for a mother's love I wanted I sought after. Unfortunately, never got that love from my mother she was lost so far from being the mother I so desired and needed. My mother was hurting and helpless, so how could she be what I needed and love me? At this point she had not truly loved herself. My mother was in search for a greater feeling, to fill the hole and lack in her own life. Being left alone a-lot I missed Mrs. Johnson so much. Her no longer being a part of my life I was just devastated I wanted so bad to have that back that love again. We wrote a few times and talked on the phone a few times. Soon quickly the calls faded and stopped. One day my mom found the sweater I had gotten from Mrs. Johnson. I slept with it every night for months missing her. My mother found it, and the cat that we at the time had peed on it. Instead of her washing it with the sheets she had taken off to clean. She threw it away. I remember coming home from school asking her where is was and her saying "I threw that S$$* away you don't need that! I remember coming home from school asking her where it was and her said "I threw that S$$* away you don't need that! She doesn't She doesn't do anything for you!" Immediately I started to cry the one thing that made me feel safe so many nights that my mother was gone, was now gone too. My mother grew more and more upset as she watched me cry and began yelling screaming, I honestly do not remember what she said other than the fact that she was really mad. Being alone so often I watched TV a whole lot I became obsessed with the show 7th heaven Because to see a family like that all together and happy was amazing to me I would, and I found myself to be so attached to the mother of the show whom reminded me of Mrs. Johnson.

Being alone so often I watched TV a whole lot I became obsessed with the show 7th heaven. Seeing a family like that all together and happy was amazing to me I would, and I found myself so attached to the mother of the show who reminded me of Mrs. Johnson. I remember she became my idol, I wanted to be just like her I also wished she were my mom. I remember she became my idol, I wanted to be just like her. I also wished she were my mom. I would often fantasize about me have a family someday having 7 kids then I said I would never be alone, and they would go to church and love God, and they would be good kids. I would often fantasize about me have a family someday, having 7 kids then I said I would never be alone, and they would go to church and love God, and they would be good kids. I would be a great mom and would give them EVERYTHING I never had. I would hold them love them, help them, when they needed it. I would have a great husband and family. At this point in my life, I remember being so angry. Now understanding life, a little bit more differently, because this love of a mother and family I wanted sought and more then I had ever wanted desired then I had ever wanted it before. My emotions really started going all over the place from angry to sad to then at times just hopeless. I began to really HATE drugs and all that they were. Somewhat hate my life I wanted to know what it was to be in a real family. One that was not in so much disorder I had had a small glimpse of what was somewhat normal with Mrs. Johnsons family in one night and I wanted that more than I had wanted anything else. Because of my true hate for drugs. I told myself will never touch them or ever go near them look at what they have done to my family.

I was left alone a-lot for days at a time somehow got use to crying myself to sleep, praying and asking God to keep me safe. But one night this night I could not sleep, and fear took over I felt like running and hiding. I felt as if my home was not safe anymore. I could not sleep so I said OK I will turn on the TV to help. Bad idea I was going through the channels and stopped on a commercial then the movie that was playing came back on. It was "Nightmare on Elm Street" I saw about 10 seconds of Freddy whom I had mentioned I was traumatized by. I wanted to crawl out of my skin. I did not know what to do I felt I as if could not breathe. I truly in my mind thought he was in my house, now mind you it was 3 am . I was so scared, and my mother of course was not there I put on clothes and ran outside. Yes, in the streets of Bed-Stuy NY at 3 am. I began walking up and down the block screaming "Ma Ma" one of her drug friends noticed me and said, "Girl what are you doing out here at this time?" I then told her I am looking for my mother she then said, "oh I 'll tell her your looking for her go back home". So, I did, she must not have been far from home because soon, she was back, and I was so scared crying just needed her a sigh of relief came over me as the door unlocked. When she walked in it was not so good. She began yelling "what the F$&@&*were you doing going out at this time of night are you crazy?! you really must want them to take you from me!!" Then, I continued to cry, even more apologizing and saying how scared I was, and I needed her. Then the look of guilt filled her face. She said, "get over here" and she hugged me and said "there was nothing to be afraid of". I then asked "can I sleep in your bed? "She said "yes". As I fell asleep, I gripped her arm and said, "please don't leave me again" she then said "you ain't got nothing to worry about I'm not going nowhere, go to sleep". I fell asleep holding her so tightly and then woke up the next morning, again with many other broken promises she was gone for another 3 days. This is where insecurity and abandonment became a part of who I was. A new deeper hurt from this moment where I put my full trust and comfort in my mother when she said she would not leave, and I was secure, then she left. This would be one of the last times for an exceptionally long time later in life that I would and will have trusted her or anyone else for that matter. Because the one person I was supposed to be able to fully trust I could no longer trust. My life was me being alone most of the time, telling lies to protect her, living a life full of broken promises. Having to become an adult because she was not there or anyone one else there to take that role as the adult in my life. Flight or fight survival mode kicked in for me, I began growing tired and angry. I would think "why do I always have to be an adult I want to be a kid for once?" I would often think of the happy and good memories, where there were no worries. Not having to think about things like will we sleep with candles tonight? Will she get grandma or grandpa to get some food? Will we have food stamps for food? when will she come home? Is she ok? These worries were a part of me now, stuck in my head like a recorded playing repeatedly. There was no

"happy" because behind that smile of mine was this constant worry. My smile was a cover, a cover for her and the madness that was really going on to cover the deep-rooted hurt that I had felt from the lack of love in my life to look normal just like a normal kid. When, I was nothing more than a hurting, love seeking little girl. But then there was the day; the day I guess I was done and ready for it to all end. I did the one thing I was told not to ever do, tell someone about what life was like, what was really happening. It was as if I did this subconsciously hoping for change. This day was a start of a change for the good, with a long and when I say long, I mean, long. A start of journey of better days a time for things to be "good" again.

As my maternal grandfather often did, he came over. My mother was his little girl whom he loves so much, he had been blinded to see he had for many years been a main source of income for my mother and her addiction. He would give her money when she asked then I think he began to see something was not right, he then started to take me to the store and let me shop for food for the house. As my mother's addiction grew, so did her need for money. To obtain the drugs she began selling the food he bought after he would leave or bring what she could back to the store. She would leave some for me just the things she could not take back. It was Saturday shopping day with my grandfather we went to the store after he came in for some coffee and as he was there, he asked me to come here he had something to tell me. I went over to him after being in my room. He and my mom were talking and having coffee. He looked at me and said, "I know your birthdays coming up soon in about a week I'm going to give your mother some money for you, ok?!?"

(You would think I would be smiling from ear to ear jumping for joy. Yes, my grandpa is going to give me money!) NO, I looked at him and said the unthinkable I guess I was fed up or just wanted justice I said, "NO Don't give it to her. She's going to use it for drugs!"

After I finished my sentence, I felt my mouth drop thinking Oh crap, did I just say that out loud? As my mouth dropped so did theirs.

My grandfather has never been told this directly he may have his suspicions.

He right away started to ask my mother questions like, "what is she talking about?!?"

My mother was furious began to deny it and protect herself saying "She doesn't know what she's talking about"! Then they began arguing some more he then walked over to me and handed me some money. Said "Here this is for you put this in a safe place", so I ran in my room and still they argued as they did, I did put it in a safe place. I just knew I had to put it somewhere where she would not find it. I taped it to the back of one of the framed pictures on my wall. Then he left and oh boy was I in for it!! But not for long. My mother had not used in a while, so she ranted and yelled at me for about 10 mins or so then she was gone. I went on with my night as I always did, being that she was often gone. I was happy; I had the money for once. I had the upper hand or so I thought. I went to bed fell asleep and sometime in the middle of the night I woke up to my room being torn apart by her and one of her drug friends. Then when he saw I was awake he said, "Esther come on where is the money I got you girl I'll give it back" because I saw right though his lying face I said, "no get out!" My mom then started screaming again about what had happened with my grandfather. Saying "how could you tell him? Now who was going to help us live, pay for the rent, pay bills? That is, it I am done! I am leaving, you and your cat can stay here, and you can figure out how the bills are going to get paid I am leaving and not coming back this time!"

I began crying and pleading for her not to leave that I needed her. She then said.

"Well, you should have thought about that before you told him that! " I had never seen her like this she was angrier than I had ever seen her. I was so scared I believed she was going to do what she said. I was only 13. I did the only thing I knew to do, called my maternal grandmother.

She also was never directly told of my mother's drug use. I believe deep down she knew; I think she did not want to believe it.

I put on cloths and walked to the corner store where the pay phone was.

My maternal grandmother had a special number where you could call her, and she would get charged for the call yea this is back for cell phones we used pay phones. So, I called her and told her about the day then told her what just happened she was not always so nice to me but underneath it I knew she loved me. then said, "hang up and call me back in a few minutes I am going to call your uncle". A few mins passed, called her again she told me she got a hold of him to go home and pack a few things he was coming to get me. I did when I got back home, my mother was back again she and her friend sitting outside. She asked me "where did you go?". I told her, then she said, "good go with her and him get out of here". Just about an hour later my uncle showed up, he was very sweet and comforting helping me get my things, my mother yelling from the other room him saying "you need to get help". We then got in his car as we drove away the tears began to fill my eyes not knowing at this point what would or was going to happen. My uncle who I was not really close to, began to reassure me. He was very heartwarming in say "baby its ok I know this is not right this is not your fault she needs help". When we got to my maternal grandmother's, who was not always the best for me to be around, she would yell at me almost all the time. She was not an affectionate person. I went upstairs and where she was and for the first time in my life, as the tears flooded my eyes, she gave me the warmest sweetest hug. I always wanted love from her, a grandmother's love and then that moment I needed it more than ever she then told me pretty much the same as my uncle did and we went to bed. The next week being my birthday, it was hard. I felt as if my whole world had been turned upside down. I was now safe, but everything I had known to be normal was not anymore. The not knowing and confusion really set in. I was somewhat relieved that I had told someone but what would happen now? A few days after that night, my mother decided to go into a rehab. Before going to the program a few days after this all happened, she stopped by my maternal grandmother's house for a visit. Wanting to see me expecting me to be happy to see her I was not I was more scared of her then I had ever been. So scared and unsure like a little puppy I hid behind my maternal grandmother. When she came up stairs and noticed how afraid I was, did not make her happy. She expected me to run into her arms, as I had done so many times before. This time was different, I remember the fear I felt knowing she was back. It was the first time I was truly afraid and had so many questions and doubts. She stayed for a little while and talked with my maternal grandmother. I hid in the next room I heard them speaking in both Spanish and English. My mother was so upset and grandmother defending me explaining again how traumatic things were for me that it would take time. She left for her 30-day program, did not see her for a while. My birthday came and you would think I would be so happy my birthday?! No, it was not. I was so hurt, and my world had been turned upside down. I still had the money my grandfather had given me, and I went out to the store the night before my birthday to feel special. I went out and bought myself balloons to bring with me to school. Most kids their parents or friends did this for them. But me, no. If I wanted to feel happy and normal as everyone else did on their birthday, I had to get them for myself. I pretended as though my home life was great when in, reality it was not. My birthday came and I went to school, got lots of happy birthdays love from teachers and friends, then headed home as the day ended. I remember having this pit in my stomach knowing what my reality at home feeling lost and alone. My maternal grandmother tried to help, she made my day better by making my favorite meal steak, mashed potatoes, and corn. A few days later my maternal grandmother happily said, "your mother's coming home", at that point I did not know what to do or how to even feel about this. It was the first time I was away from her so long. With it being such at traumatic separation I had lost all trust and hope in her. Did not know how to feel, who was she now or would she be. The day came she finished her program and was headed home. This overwhelming feeling of fear came over me. When my maternal grandmother told me, I asked her if I could stay for a while longer until I was ready. My maternal grandmother then said, "you can stay as long as you need to". When my mother heard this, it was upsetting for her, now being clean she was a-little more understanding and was ok with it. We had to take baby steps in spending time together little by little, we would go out to lunch together, movies small things like that. After getting out of detox, she joined a rehab program. she was getting better, and things were looking up. Just as things were looking up, she got devastating news that would be the start of a long journey that would change our lives forever!

# CHAPTER 5

# PIECES OF DEVASTATION & FEAR

This was when we found out my mother was extremely sick. After she fought and worked so hard to get clean from drug use. She now had another battle to fight, LUNG CANCER! Just as I thought maybe, just maybe things could be better, we could grow as a family. Thinking my mom was better, then finding out just as she had turned one sickness around, she had now gained another. This feeling of fear and devastation fell over on me almost immediately as I heard this news. I was so upset thought I was going to have my mother, the mother I always longed for with nothing in the way, well nope not me. I remember thinking WHY ME?! God what did I do to deserve this? Drugs took her time and attention away from me and now lung cancer? Our extended family found out she now had cancer. They lived in Tampa Florida, knew of great doctors Oncologist. Advised my mother that they were some of the best Oncologist. My mother then decided it was time to move again on to Florida again this time, Tampa. My mother had been attending a drug program. She decided we would move after she graduated from the program. Around this time, we found some good news; my sister was pregnant. She was still living in Florida, (South Florida). When my sister heard the news, we were moving to Tampa, she decided to move to be with us. All these things seemed great, amazing things to look forward to. Of course, though there was still this little yet big life changing thing called cancer. This devastating news took all that joy out of all our lives, the consent not knowing. Although we would all be together again after so long. My mother was finally clean of drug use, she now once again have to fight. As soon she could to start treatment she did. She found an oncologist, found a place for us to live. She was off to Florida. Leaving me back in New York with my maternal grandmother till the end of that school year.

Off Florida to start a new life filled with hope but, yet devastation. I was overly concerned for my mother and her condition. I was now faced with the fact that I could lose my mother now this time forever. With my mother's condition needing all the help and support she could get. Not long after me moving to Florida a few weeks later my maternal grandmother and uncle would join us. My maternal Grandfather stayed living in New York. This meant my maternal grandmother would sell her home, after so many years of having the house. I grew up in, on and off but the place I called home for many years was now being sold. My maternal grandmother also had another daughter who stayed in New York with her husband and three children. Who had a life established there that they could not leave. There were a lot of my family and friends that we left behind this was a little sad, I understood it was the best for my mother. She would go to one of the best facilities in the country, helping her fighting this new battle. She did not just fight this with medications, she fought with prayer. She was far from perfect, but she did grow up knowing God and who He was and knew who turn to when she needed help. I believe He was there with her though this battle for her life. Shortly after moving Florida my mother started her Chemo treatment. She was so sick it scared me. I really thought my mother was so sick that this was it, we did not have much time left with her. She was very weak her hair began coming out. She was heavily sedated at times from the medication, especially at bedtime she would take the heaviest medications to help her sleep. My sister and her husband came to live with us. About a week later my uncle and maternal grandmother also moved in. All together in a two-bedroom one bath apartment. Now this was six people and also a 60-pound dog living in and small two-bedroom apartment. To say in nicely it was CRAZY to say the very least. My maternal grandmother and uncle had started the process of buying their new home in Florida. My sister and husband also looked for a place. Eventually it became too much with all of us in this small place pushing my uncle and maternal grandmother went to a hotel until their home was ready. My sister had only been living with us for about a month, when she was then put on bed rest and had to stay in the hospital two months until the baby was born.

The Summer came to an end, I started my first year of high school. Here, I was again the "new girl" this I was used to, but it was not always easy. After I was registered, I was given a time and place to take a school bus. It didn't make me very happy being that every morning for the next year, I would wake up <u>at 5 am</u> every day to walk to a bus stop in the dark by <u>6 am.</u> It was only a few blocks away but still very dark, the first few mornings my mother drove me. I met a friend Holly, who had lived nearby with her grandparents. Holly and I clicked right away, even though she was a year older than me. We walked to the bus together every morning. We became close quickly, doing things outside of school and I also got to know both of her grandparents. They began treating me as if I were one of their own. I went over most afternoons after school; I spent a lot of time with them. Holly and I where became very close over time. Then one morning would change both of our lives forever. When moving to this area my mother not really know the Tampa area, we soon found out that this area was not the best of areas to live. One morning walking to the bus stop with Holly, we noticed a strange man, we would always see people who had seemed to be on drugs, but we would just ignore them, and they never really bothered us. This guy was acting even more out of the ordinary. He had said things like "Hey girls " before and we would just ignore him, and he would leave us alone. Until this morning, he first came up to us on a bike saying inappropriate sexual comments (no need to repeat them). Just after he passed the bus showed up and we quickly got on in hopes that we would never see him again. Neither one of us had told anyone, other than friends at school. Then the next morning we were extremely cautious while walking to the bus stop, hoping we would not see him Again. As we walked, we looked around and did not see him and boy were we happy. Just as we said to one another how relieved we were. He road by again on his bike saying those things again. Then he was gone, and we were relieved again we thought ok he's gone. We started talking and I glanced down the street. To my surprise, saw him with himself exposed touching himself staring at us. We turned around right away and were even more afraid now. Saying, "if he was bold enough to do that what else mite he do?" then he then began walking toward us. As he did the bus started come down the street and he turned around. We got on the bus and as soon as we got to school, we told our school counselor. Then the police got involved, for the next few mornings we had a cop car patrolling our bus stop area. Thankfully eventually he was caught and brought to jail.

It had been about two months and my sister had been in the hospital on bed rest. The time had come for my nephew to arrive. My sister living with us meant I would be there and with her for his birth. Even with my mother going through her treatment she was still very excited for this moment and somehow had enough strength to go through it all with her. My sister was in a whole lot of pain I remember asking her if I could do anything to help and she turned around as if I was the one hurting her and screamed "NO!" This was and understandable response, her being in so much pain. So, there we all were in the room with her and yup for the first time I saw what childbirth was and how beautifully gross it is. Then there he was this beautifully created little baby, the love that quickly grew in my heart was amazing. I never knew I could ever love someone or thing so much, he became a great distraction from reality of everything. He became the light the light in my world of darkness. Although

I had him to bring such joy and love I had never known, I still had feelings of depression that never went away. From dealing with the lack of a healthy childhood that was stolen. Also, with my mother's condition I felt even more hopeless now, knowing there was nothing anyone could do. All we could do was hope and pray that the medicine worked. Dealing with my life was not the easiest as you could imagine, and I became an incredibly angry bitter child.

The 9th grade continued I at least still had Holly who had become my best friend. We had so much in common we had so many great times together it felt great to not feel so alone for once. In this time of me being so angry a bit of rebellion started to set in as well.

I was not a pleasant student for some of my teachers, I loved some teachers but others I was just downright nasty to. The other friends I choose were not the best choices I could have made either. They were just as hurt and broken as I was. Somehow even with me choosing these friends, I was the good girl of the group because a lot of them where doing things that were much worse, than I would have ever done. Also doing things that were way more mature for our age of 15 then they should have been doing. Within the circle of friends, I was considered the "Good girl" because I had a limit to the things I would do. I was in the stage "I'm gonna hurt you before you hurt me".

There were clearly kids and teachers I liked and liked me and other teachers I had no respect for whom I did not treat well. It was the same with peers just some kids who I did not get along with. This is not something I am proud of in anyway at all. Although I understand why I was this way, I was just broken and hurting dealing with so much carrying a very heavy load. The year was coming closer to an end. Suddenly just before it ended something unthinkable, and terrifying happened. As I had mentioned I got up every morning for school <u>at 5 am</u> . I woke up as if it were any other morning and went into the shower. I remembered walking pass the electric breaker box and seeing it was open. Thought nothing of it, when I was in the shower I remember feeling as though someone was watching me, but I had often felt like that being traumatized as a child fear. I thought it was just me, something I would often feel. It was a normal to me to feel that kind of fear. I got out of the shower and went to my dresser for undergarments. My dresser was tall and inside my closet. The doors had been taken off (mind you I was completely naked and vulnerable) the closet went deep to the left with a wall covering it beyond the opening. My dresser was in the closet and still there was room for hangers. It was hard to see beyond the hangers where the closet continued. Beyond the opening to the closet there was quite a bit of room to store things. We had a futon mattress was stored in the back there with room left over. Now you must be thinking why so much detail about such small and unmeaningful things? well there is a reason for me explaining this. I want you to really get the picture of it all. After getting my undergarments I then put them on and went to get clothes for school that were clean in a basket by the window. Now mind you, I just got out of the shower dried myself, but was still a little damp. As I looked though the clothes, I felt a cold breeze, then noticed the window was open. I thought it was odd but continued to dress. It did not raise any red flags I just went on with my morning thinking maybe my mom had opened the window. Then thought (why would she open my window?) I went into my mother's room and asked, " Did you open my window?" Now just think it is probably at least 5:15 am by this point not the time to mess with her. She began yelling "What Do you mean your window is open get out!" I went back to my room across the hall the bathroom separated her room from mine I went back over to the basket by the window she was still yelling because I had gone in her room. I was so calm; (I remember so clearly just putting on my cloths) talking to her saying "well maybe someone is stalking us" (laughed a little). She then called me into her room softly saying this time "What do you mean your window is open?" I then said " Its open. I do not know how. I did not open It. I thought you did" she then said, "I didn't open it so how did it get open?" this was the moment she realized that there was something wrong. I then again said "I do not know I have to go finish getting ready for school" walked back to my room. Then again, she a few mins later she calls me back to her room, and with the most con-fused look on her face says, "what do you mean your windows open and you didn't open it because I didn't" I then looked at her and said "You want to go look its open and no I didn't open it" She then said out of nowhere, said "go check your closet". Having always dealt with fear, I did not want to go and look but tried to listen. I walked to the edge of my doorway and a feeling of fear just swept through me from head toe. I could not bring myself to go in. I turned around and said to my mother "No I don't want to" She then Yelled "I don't know why, your being so scared. If there is someone in there, I'll shoot them with my Nine" (meaning a nine-millimeter gun that she really didn't have).

I then went back to the edge of my doorway. As I stepped into my room, I saw a man coming toward me from out of the deep part of my closet with a ski mask and gloves on. I freaked out to say the very least I turned around ran into my mother's room and jumped on top of her saying "there's someone in there, there's someone in there !!" She had to fight me and the covers off her she somehow grabbed a hammer. She saw him run and turn the corner near my bedroom going into the kitchen. He was running toward the back door trying to get out thinking she really had a gun. He must have known our apartment layout and because he knew just where the back door was. I was still in my mom's room hiding poking my head out occasionally. I heard lots of banging and things being thrown not knowing what was going on I thought it was a fight. It caused me to go into a panic even more. Later I heard the rest of this story from my mother. As I was hiding in the room. The sound of what I thought was a struggle was my mother throwing oranges that were on the table as she screamed "get out!" She was waving the hammer the guy thought was a gun.

I can just picture this happening (it makes me laugh a little now)

the only funny part of this story might I add. I can just picture my mother throwing oranges at the guy and waving the hammer she had in her other hand, that the guy thinks is a gun. I cannot help but wonder what must have been going through his head. As funny as this may have been to imagine, this was so scary, and I really felt as though God protected my mother and myself. My mother later told me, for her one of the scariest moments for her was, when he was attempting to get out, trying to unlock the door he stopped for a moment, turned around and looked right at her. It was scary for her because when he did this, she could not see his face. After he looked at her, he then unlocked the door and left. I then got on the phone with 911 and it took over 45 min for the police to show up.

After this happened of course we could not stay in this home. Until we could find a new place to live it was off to my maternal grandmother's where her and my uncle where and uncle were living. I was not thrilled about living with there, but I do remember I was happy thinking that I would never have to sleep in that house. It was not easy living with my maternal grandmother. She was starting to get Alzheimer's. Unfortunately, I was her target for her anger and confusion. If something happened, it somehow became my fault. To say the least, I was not very happy about the move, but we had a roof over our heads my mother said so that's all that mattered.

At times life literally felt like hell on earth. I was 15, I began to really sink into depression and sadness. I was constantly told I was not going to amount to anything. How my existence as a person was worthless. I remember Just wanting so badly an escape. I remember clearly this was when suicidal thoughts started to creep in. Sadness and heaviness were growing on me like mold slowly growing clouding and covering any amount of joy and happiness I felt or had at all. It was like depression over the years had become like mold. Just as mold grows on a wall on a moist wall slowly but deadly growing. It was always slowly growing slowly taking over in time with no help. My family was not helpful at all. I remember feeling like I was not ever heard as if I were in a movie, where a person dies, and they come back as a (ghost spirt) and there standing in front of the ones they love screaming at the top of their lungs, but their loved ones cannot hear or see them because they died. Well, that is how I felt. As if I was in a room screaming at the top of my lungs filled with people that were supposed to love me. Yet no one was listening, and no one could hear me, I wanted to feel and be important and to be accepted. Wanting a father and mother to give all the love my heart longed for. I was shouting help emotionally, screaming I am drowning, from your hurtful words the lack of love, care, and concern. But there was no answer. I was calling out for someone to save me, yet it was like I was that ghost in the movie unheard. Even for this short time living with my maternal grandmother was not good for me. I had about a week or so before the summer started. Then I was there all day long to endure it all, all the time. As I explained she did always treat me the best as a young child, now with her confusion and anger because of the Alzheimer's. As a teen it was not any better but much worse. With my maternal grandmother having to receive more help even at times, that help coming from me. That shot her confidence down and I was the target for her anger. I sadly Believe from her actions. She would constantly tell me how dumb and worthless I was in her eyes. When I did help, I never could do things right, she always found something that was wrong, it was not exactly right. Dealing with depression another way I found to fill the void of hurt I ate. It was comforting to me, as a result I gained quite a bit of weight. So, let's just say I wasn't the skinniest teen at the age of 15. Just about my whole family but my maternal grandmother and uncle were the worst of them all, made fun of me and I got the constant fat jokes and comments. Living with them was not easy I became the butt of the jokes. I would go into the refrigerator to get something out of the fridge to eat or drink. Even if they had no Idea what I was going into the fridge for. It did not matter it would be one of two things that would happen always consistent basis. Either I'd get a dirty look and snare, I would be told things like" What are you going into the refrigerator for your already fat, you don't need any more food" or " ha ha what are you going in there for?", "get out you have enough fat to last you a week", "you can go without maybe you 'll lose some weight" . These words cut deeper and deeper every time they were said. These were the things they did not realize that made that mold aka depression grow more covering me until I felt like I was suffering. The crazy part in all of this, they saw this as normal. They thought the things that were said to me were ok, normal to say or even funny. They never knew or realized how much it hurt and affected my life and value of who I was. Living there was also hard because it was in the middle of nowhere in the country on an acre of land. I had no friends; I was alone and there with maternal grandmother and uncle. My mother had not always there and just allowed them to treat me that way. She maybe once or twice tried to defend me but failed. She was not any help, she let it happen she would laugh with them then ask them to stop. My mom and I had nowhere to go and that was home, she had her chemo treatments to worry about and keeping herself heathy. She was also Working to try to get a new place for us to live. I felt more helpless and vulnerable day in and out. I was constantly being preyed on by my own family the ones who are supposed to protect me and make me feel safe. I dealt with it as long as I could until one day, I felt I couldn't, I thought can't take this anymore, anywhere has got to be better than this reality, I was living in. I decided in a moment of anger, filled with bitterness and sadness that had been built up for many years of my life, along with a long battle of loneliness and depression. In this point of life for me, I had been through more than most have ever had to deal with in their entire lives.

I had an argument with my grandmother I sometimes tried to fight back verbally and defend myself although I never won. I was 15 and treated as a 5-year-old. She dragged me by my ponytail to my room and told me to stay there, until she told me to come out. She did this often and I knew until when I was sent to my room it could be the rest of the day. To be completely honest, I do not even remember what the reason was and what we even were arguing about. I was 15 sent to a room with only 4 walls and clothes she had taken the TV away if I had a drawing pad, I was lucky. I remember bawling my eyes out thinking I just CAN'T take this anymore I cannot live like this. I had been so excited because my brother and sister-in-law were coming up from Fort Lauderdale. For the weekend with my niece and nephew. A break from all the chaos I remember thinking. My brother made a different life for him and his family, they were very much different than ours happy and healthy. Now I was being shut out from the little bit of excitement I had left in life at this point growing up I did not have a lot of time with my brother. He had moved away when I was young, so I really did not get to see he much. This was a something I was so looking forward to, was now being taken. At this time my father would and did

53

fade in and out of my life, I would call him every now and then, but he wasn't present or around. In this moment of uncontrollable sadness and cloudiness of the mold of depression hearing thoughts of worthlessness in mind. I made the decision in that moment of being thrown into my room that life was just bad, and it wasn't ever gonna get any better. I went into my closet got a wired hanger and rapped it around my neck and decided, that's it I'm going to take my life. I pulled and pulled and pulled while sobbing and as I felt my breath leave, I said "GOD PLEASE JUST TAKE ME!" I remember it so clearly till this day, I heard a voice say NO and as soon as I heard I let go gasping for air. I then sobbed saying why, why. After about an hour or so I went out into the bathroom and looked at myself in the mirror. I had huge bruises on two areas of my neck where the hanger had been. I remember as I looked into the mirror, watching the tears fall as if I were in a dream or in a state of slow motion. I wish I could say after this, things got better, that somehow my family after seeing what I had tried to do that would have opened there eyes somehow. I would no longer be the ghost in that room screaming with no one listening but unfortunately things just got even worse. I never forget the moment of walking to see if I could come out of my room and silently screaming HELP with the bruises on my neck. I went on to the patio where most of my family members were standing before them with bruises that were less then unnoticeable. For once I had everyone's attention, right? The room went silent, my mother looked at me in shock, said "What were u thinking?" "Are you an idiot?" I then had my uncle look at me and said, "Oh you want to kill yourself?" "Next time if you try and you use a knife do not cut across cut the other way, so you get the vein". My maternal grandmother then said, "OK that is what you want to do? we'll call the cops and then to take you to the crazy house". My sister-in-law came into the room after hearing the things that were being said, she rushed and got my brother who was in another part of the house. He grabbed me took me to another part of the house, he began asking me why? why would you do something like that? sobbing told him why and just how I was feeling. He and his wife were so upset, they just could not believe how bad things were, that it had come to that. Being that it was still summer for two more weeks until school started after their visit. My brother told my mother he was taking me home with him for the rest of the summer, because him and his wife were concerned about me. They took me back to Fort Lauderdale with them for the rest of that summer.

The summer ended and my mother found a new place for us to live. I was in a different town Oldsmar, still close to Tampa but in a new place. This meant another new high school, Tarpon Springs High. I was extremely excited to be moving, this was the most excitement I had about moving in a very long time. My life to somewhat be just a little bit easier. Where it was just me and my mom life was no picnic at times living with her ether but at least it was just her. She was still going through her treatments for chemotherapy. This time slowly became the scariest of all times in my life because shortly after we moved, she began to get sicker. As I mentioned before, my mother grew up in a church a Pentecostal background. We would off and on growing up go to church when in New York we would attend a church my grandfather was very dedicated to and attended weekly. In

Florida we would try different churches but my mother in the same way we moved never stayed anywhere too long this is what happened with churches we never stayed anywhere too long. My mother heard of a church in Tampa where the preacher had a God given gift of healing. Until this point, I had ever heard or seen anything like this. As soon as my mother heard of this, she said she had to go and check this church out. We did I remember being so nervous, not knowing anyone or knowing what was going to happen. The service was like a lot of other places we had gone but at the end people were asked if you have a sickness or need prayer to come up to the front of the alter. When the time came my mother went up, I remember saying a prayer for her as my mother was being prayed. I was also hoping and praying asking Him to heal her. No matter what had happened how she treated me I did not want to lose her. (I had hoped the prayer worked but I had never seen or heard of anything like it before.) She had a doctor's appointment the next week, the doctors did some test on her to see the progress of her getting her treatments if getting better or possibly worse. She was asked to come back a week or so later for the results. The day of the next follow up appointment, it was that day that changed my thoughts about God, who He was, what He can and will do for those who believe in him! The doctors were Amazed saying that they had never seen anything like it before. They had great news the cancer was Gone! I now understand what God does and how He works but at the time I did not even fathom or understand what he had done. Thirteen years later while writing this truly. I can grasp and appreciate what he did in saving her life. It was truly a miracle; I remember being happy knowing her life was not going to end. By the grace of God, she was still alive! Not just alive but cancer free! Now that my mother was on the road to recovery and getting her health back in order What was lifelike? better? different? ... I wish! I could say that but unfortunately, I cannot say any of those things. As she got better the screaming, did not stop nor did the pain I had felt constantly. Did not go away I really wish it did, but it did not. Unfortunately, as her health increase the verbal abuse did not stop.

I was constantly called things like, "you are so stupid, you Dumb B***" and so much more. I could not understand why the abuse did not stop. She was drug free and cancer free. I mean I should be slowly gaining a heathy mother inside and out right? No although she was healed, she still was her "normal" if not worse. It just became normal again I used my best coping method at the time and that was to eat. Eating now that made me happy, it was my one free coping mechanism.

My sister would visit often even stay for periods of time. I loved and I mean loved spending time with my nephew. Also, many times help taking care of him the love that grew in my heart for him was unexplainable. I felt a love from him for me that I had never known, he loved me without condition. He loved me for me, I began to live for this love. With all that I had gone through did not have much of that. I loved him so much if feel as though he was brought into this world to save my life. He truly became the light of my world. Having him around gave me hope for the future, a future that was filled with hope and happiness. It was as if God was using him to allow my love for children to grow it was because for my love for him. I later realized I wanted to love and care for children. I dreamed of the day that I would be happy and that it would all end. When I was old enough, I would get out of there, get out of that atmosphere and I would not look back.

I was now in my 10th grade year of high school I had calmed down a whole lot from my first year of high school. I was again drawn to the broken hurting kids in school like me. I know now, that the hurting no matter what shape size or color you are, flock together. Because really the "bad Kids " as they call them.

(Really just hurting kids if you ask me). We are the way we are for a reason. (a nasty person is not that way because they want to be. I am sure people who are rude, and nasty do not wake up in the morning and say ok today I am gonna be extra nasty because I like it. No, there is always a reason why people are the way they are especially when it comes to children. Yes, even teens what they have been taught an or not taught. Things such as if there was love or if there was not and if not all most of these so called "bad kids" just need love. When God made us, we were made in his image and one of our greatest needs is love.

"What a person desires is unfailing love"
Proverbs19:22 NIV

For me, the lack of love meant, and I did not know how to love the way I was meant to love. Because of this deep desire to be love that I craved. I did not always act in away a normal teen would. Anyone who showed attention, and affection I would cling to. I always wanted to be around those who showed me any kind of love and attention in an unhealthy unbalanced way.

I did not really understand boundaries. I believe it was because love was not something often given to me as a child. When it was given to me, I somehow lost the person who gave me affection and attention. I believe I subconsciously acted in an unhealthy manner. I believe it was me trying to somehow control a part of my life that meant so much in my world full of chaos and disfunction. So, I did not respect boundaries or understand that at times people need their space and even if someone loved you, they needed other people, friends, and responsibilities in their lives, and I was not the center. I never understood or was taught balance I basically raised myself. This was concept was something I did not understand. I became that sweet but annoying teenager who was hurting so bad, I just needed and wanted to be loved. When I received love, I wanted to be in control, so it would not go away. Which in fact I had no idea that my innocent intentions would, do the exact opposite. Especially with one teacher. There were not many people I did this with but there were a few. I have already told the story of Mrs. Johnson. I had longed for that same love and relationship once again. In moving to this new school there was a teacher that reminded me of Mrs. Johnson. She had blond hair and blue eyes just like her let's call her Mrs. "W". She was just as sweet or so I thought, and down to earth as Mrs. Johnson. Let's Just say If I had known what I know now I think would have things would have turned out differently. How many times do we say or hear the saying "if I knew what I knew now than" but life's full of lessons. To be honest I wished I did not have to go through some of the things I did. Unfortunately, I cannot change what happened.

Before I go any further with this story about Mrs. "W" I must stop and say this, any trained adult teaching children should understand the signs of a child like me, that I clearly was going through something and there was something deeply wrong. This coming from me, a now trained teacher working with children for more than 16 years. I know the signs or an abused or deeply hurting child.

Back to the story, I began to look this teacher for love and affection. I confided in her. I opened up to her, telling her all that I had been through. I was looking for someone to fix me, to love me. I soon found out I had chosen the wrong person. Although she was genuinely nice and seemed to be loving and understanding, down to earth even. I did spend quite bit of my extra time in her classroom after class, talking and helping her. So, could this have been a little annoying yeah, I am sure, to an untrained person. I was not taught. So really what did I know? this was normal for me. I wanted love and I went about it in the only way I knew. One day would change everything. While in a class connected to another teacher's class, I was there working on an assignment during lunch waiting for my next class to start. Mrs. "W" was in the other class that was connected to where I was. Talking to My other teacher, she did not know I was in the next room. I overheard their conversation. The other teacher asked, "How's Esther Doing?", Mrs. "W" says "Man I'm gonna need some preparation H I just can't get rid of her" then was laughter from both teachers as well as assistants. This was so devastating for me to hear, a sixteen-year-old broken kid who only trusted a few people. Hearing her say those words, as if I meant nothing and was a running joke, it was like knives into my heart. Just another person I trusted hurting me. I was filled with anger and sadness all at once. I threw something across the room after hearing her say this. I then grabbed my things, as I did another teacher came in the room. Stormed quickly, then heard someone yell, "Esther wait!!!" It just so happened to be time to go to my next class. This part is a bit comical, out of all places my next class was Drama! It was fitting for the next thing that occurred. I went into the class crying. Of course, the teacher (who I might add was sincerely sweet) came over to me asking what was wrong. This poor teacher who, I remember was very petite. She had to deal with me, with so much anger and hurt, it became overwhelming as I began explaining what happened. As anger continued to build, I started throwing things. Then she tried to calm me down she took me out the side door from the classroom. I began yelling and screaming, I was so angry I looked over at a stack of chairs in the classroom door, I pushed her aside going back into the classroom. I picked up a chair put it up over my head. I began yelling "I should go hit that B@#@ with this" As little as she was, she got in my face yelling at me, saying "Put the chair down!" She would have to call the school officer. I said OK, but how did I put it down? I threw it on the grass! After I did, I took some time to myself crying alone. She came over and hugged me saying she was so sorry, take my time to cool down and everything would be ok. After this happened, to say the least, I was not happy. I wish I could say that this was the last time this kind of thing happened in the sense of a teacher doing something that humiliated me. But it was not on top of all my emotional issues, I also dealt with a learning disability. I learned a bit different. Instead of hearing the directions once, I had to hear it more than once, I just learned things differently.

Unfortunately, I had another teacher who was not understanding when it came to me having a learning disability. He was a very cocky jerk to say the least. He was the school's football coach and a teacher. One day in math class, math being one of my hardest subjects, he explained how to solve an algebra problem. I did not understand, so I asked again. He explained one more time. Unfortunately, I still did not understand, just as he was sitting down, I raised my hand again. He then got up in front of the whole class, took a book and slammed it on my desk. He then said, "You must have some blonde underneath all of that brown hair!" in front of the entire class. After this, I struggled in school because I never asked a teacher a question again. Nor did it help with my view on male authority, which was already distorted because of my father.

My High School year continued the summer came and went. Depression continued to grow, sadness and the longing for change that never came. One of my teachers noticed something was wrong and recommend me to see the guidance counselor. So, I began seeing her and talking with her about many things, one being depression. One day, in a cry for help I told her something that made her worry. She knew in the past I had tried to take my life. I went to her upset really dealing with a heavy sadness. I mentioned that my mom was away for the weekend, I was sad feeling alone. She asked me a few questions then said to me, "I do not know if I feel comfortable sending you home in this depressed state. Not knowing if you will try and take your life again, with no one being at home over the weekend. Is there any place you can go?" I told her "No" that I would be "fine". She was not convinced. The next thing I knew, at seventeen I was now being taken to a hospital where I was "baker acted" for depression and suicidal thoughts. I remember being so angry at her because once again someone that I trusted had said they cared about me. (At the time, my eyes - made things worse as an adult I understand her prospective and why she did what she did) I then was taken by a school police officer, handcuffed into the back of his car as if I were a criminal. I remember being so afraid and bawling my eyes out the entire time. I then made it to the hospital and from there I remember just seeing doctor after doctor and talking hours on end. I was there for a few days and given medications. It all seems like such a big blur, but there are key things I remember. My mom showing up is disbelief this was happening, though she knew that I had tried taking my life in the past. It was there at the hospital that for the first time I felt I was heard. For the first time, the mention of emotional abuse was brought to her attention although she denied it. The doctor talked about how he knew from the stories told that I was being emotionally abused. Of course, I was portrayed to be a liar and I had the best life that I was not being abused at all. She told the doctor, "I give her everything she needs, she does not know what real abuse is". After a few days I was taken home and I just remember the feeling of sadness and loneliness yet again just became a part of me as if it were normal. The fighting and arguing at home did not stop. Being constantly told "You are nothing" and "You will never be anything important". Oh that, that continued. During this time, my mother started to date an old boyfriend from the past. She began using drugs again, she relapsed. She was angrier than ever blaming anything and everything that she could on me. The thoughts of suicide began to just continue to get worse in a month of being home. The only thing that seemed to make me happy was being around my nephew. That is the only happiness at that time in my life. His innocence just gripped my heart, and his smile brightened my day. In some ways, I feel as if he saved me, he was the only thing that made me want to live.

Around this time, I received a life changing letter. A couple years prior when we moved back to Tampa, I had written to Mrs. Johnson. I still had her address from all those years prior. I had kept all of Mrs. Johnsons letters; I found the letters in the move. I mailed her a letter not receiving a response, I guess I let it go. Now this being a few years later I got a letter back from her. I do not really know how she found this new address from the old one, but she did! I remember crying as I read each word, I had sent the letter to an old address of hers she did not get it for a long time, she explained in the letter. She said she was so happy to hear from me. My heart was filled with so much Joy, here she was again in my life. It was such an awful time, just when I needed her most, she was back again. She left her phone number and asked me to call. I did we talked every now and then. She told me about her life and how things had Changed she now had another daughter 2 years old, and she had remarried. I told her about the one good happy exciting thing in my life my nephew. During the summer as we stayed in touch, talking on the phone and writing. She, with my mother's permission of course, invited me to come visit her in South Florida, about 4-5 hours from where I lived in Oldsmar FL. A soon as I got the ok from my mother I found away! I got a greyhound bus ticket. I was so nervous and excited all at the same time. I loved Norah Jones, being that I heard on of her songs for the first time in Mrs. Johnsons car years before. I had my CD player with me I listened to Norah Jones the whole ride. After a long drive the time came, I was there, it was genuinely like a movie, I had so much excitement just the thought of one full week of feeing loved. In, a peaceful and joy filled environment. I left the place I called home, leaving all the hurtful words the mental abuse and physical abuse behind.

As the bus pulled in the station and I saw her, I remember shaking like a leaf and tearing up almost in unbelief. That this was not a dream this was really happening. I got off the bus and ran into her arms we both cried in excitement. That hug has never left me, a loving hug from such a warmhearted person that made one of the biggest impacts in my life. (Even writing this now my eyes fill with tears feeling all those same emotions all over again. The love in my heart for her even all these years later has not changed.) On the drive back to her house she told me of all the plans she had for us. She knew just how much I loved the beach, she did too. She had her now two-year-old daughter, she was so excited for me to meet and her husband of course. It was truly the most excited I had been in such a long time. It was such a memorable time; I remember thinking I never want to leave. Just think of the atmosphere I had come from, going into such a different one. I remember thinking why my life, could not have always been this amazing, filled with nothing but love and happiness. The next day, we went on her husband's boat. This was my first time ever being on a boat I was so nervous. I got up the courage to jump off the boat in the middle of the ocean looking down freaking out because I only saw the blue dark ocean. Getting back on the boat so quickly thinking I was going to get eaten by a shark. Then her husband took me to a place in the ocean that was about 15 feet deep I could see everything. I went snorkeling it was nice until out of a long tunnel came out a huge eel. I put on the speed again in swimming back to the boat because if not I was going to get stung or eaten in my mind and let's face it, it's a big snake in the ocean. We had a good laugh when I got back on the boat. The rest of my time there, I spent time with her daughter who was my nephew's age. She was such a sweet cute little girl, as much as I could not get enough of playing with her, she seemed to have the same feelings about me. There where so many memorable moments from fun playing times with her daughter, going to the beach, and even a Ketchup fight in the kitchen between Mrs. Johnson and me. Those moments where great, but my favorite moments were, her telling me goodnight giving me the sweetest hug and standing at the door asking me if I was, ok? Asking if needed and needed anything else? Me answering no. Then her turning off the light with a smile saying goodnight. I was seeing and feeling a mother's love for first time the way it should be. Then waking up and opening my eyes seeing this big smile on her face, then her saying "it is time to wake up". Then asking, "how did I sleep?" Me answer great then her say "come out that she had made breakfast". (These simple moments that may just seem so normal, to me they were everything because my whole life I had never had someone be so kind and attentive) Last, but not least favorite moment was our one-on-one talks on her back porch. I was on one of those days, I for the first time told her everything, everything I was always told not to tell. I began telling her all my struggles she had not known about. All this time I had to raise myself how emotionally I was affected by it. This was at the end of our week together, I was torn up devastated I did not want to ever leave, let alone the next day. It was still summer, I had to go back to being alone being abused emotionally with no escape. I told her how I felt about going home and remember telling her I might just take my life. If I had gone home, asking her to stay longer. Although the thoughts of suicide did and were incredibly strong, being there was so amazing, for me this like leaving heaven literally. Going right back into Hell that was my life, how I just could not leave. Even though this is true it was how I was feeling I remember hoping that she would feel the desperateness in me and let me stay longer. (I now know and understand as an adult I used my feelings as a way of manipulation to stay longer.)I just remember feeling this desperate feeling of never wanting to leave. Here I was again thinking that is it I will lose her again. Clearly although I was older, I was still very broken. She then asked me to call my mother asking if I could stay longer, so I did. My mother said yes and stayed for another week. Another week of happiness I thought, it was yet another week full of love and so much laughter. It all eventually came to an end though I cried at the thought of leaving but I knew I had to. (Writing this now I feel so bad for using manipulation to stay longer, although I was struggling with thoughts of suicide, I now know even in desperation I was wrong. Using it so she would feel bad, although I did truly feel that way. I think now as an adult of the pressure and worry

I must have put on her. Someone who did not deserve such pressure I understand the child in me and why I did what I did but it was not ok.) I wish I could say things got better for me after leaving there but they did not. It was time she drove me to the bus station gave me the biggest warmest hug. On the bus I went, as it drove off, I remember so clearly, literally sobbing all the way home. Crying myself to sleep in fact, waking up at stop. Then turning on music again, while still crying. I got home things where just like I had never left. I remember my mother having an attitude and was upset because she could tell I was not happy when I arrived home.

Here is a good analogy to help you understand a little better emotionally how I was feeling. Think food, it is a need in life, right? If we do not get enough of it so many things can go wrong. People who are hungry become what? Desperate, angry, and irritable. Our bodies need food it is something we cannot live without. What do hungry starving people do almost any-thing to get food. When then they get it, the body even gets des-perate and begins to store it, not knowing when it will get food next. Now let's think of a child and their needs. A child needs to be loved and nurtured to grow; it is like emotional food. This is a need we are all created with, created in God's image.

> "So, God created mankind in his own image, in the image of God he created them; male and female he created them." Genesis 1:27 NIV

We were created this way it is a vial desire from the very start of our lives.

68

Now with this being the way we were created that understanding being clear. Emotionally for me this "food" Love was a lack from me, and I finally got it. In my visit with Mrs. Johnson. Because I had always lost her once before and so many others. I was going home not knowing when and If I would ever see her again. It was completely devastating. It was having that emotional food ripped right out of my hands. With all that said, going home where I knew that love was not, and never was. This did not make it easy for me in the least. As much as it helped visiting with Mrs. Johnson, it hurt so bad leaving. I kept in touch with her through letters and phone calls. As my depression grew living back in this environment with no emotional help. I grew desperate I just wanted out; the thoughts of suicide began to get stronger all over again.

(Still to this day, how I explain having suicidal thoughts is, it is like being on fire emotionally. You want to end the pain, just as a person who is physically on fire will in desperation want to stop burring physically. In the same way, in the moment of wanting the emotional pain to stop, the only way out you see is to end your life.)

As these feelings began to continue, I remember Mrs. Johnson calling me, I went into my grandmothers' room into her closet. Sat on the floor I spoke to her. Told her exactly how I felt, the deep thoughts I had been feeling, her saying something like, you cannot keep saying "I'm not going to be able to talk to you anymore". I began crying feeling hopeless. The one person who cared I thought now didn't any longer. I came out of the closet with tears in my eyes my mother nastily said, "uh what are you crying for?" I then looked up and there was my nephew walking over to me with a big smile on his face, I melted. He always had a way of making everything I was feeling fade. Nothing else seem to matter but him when he was a round, I could drown out all the harsh words and emotional stabs. That was the last time I spoke to Mrs. Johnson. For years sadness and anger built, she became just another person in my life who said she cared and then failed me. It was my fault not really hers, I was broken no one really wanted me or wanted to love me. I have always since I can remember, thought this was way. This was normal to me; I had no reason to think differently. There is always and always will be a soft place in my heart for her she made a huge impact on my life. I will be forever grateful I have and kept all her letters; in a memory box I keep I often look back through and will always hold her in my heart.

(I see and understand this completely now as an adult, I look at it from Mrs. Johnsons perspective. I put her in an impossible position, I was still a young child that was miles away. She could not do anything to help me. What if I had gone through with taking my life the way I had said and felt? How would she feel? At the time I felt that she did not care. Really, she did, what she did by loosing contact because she cared so much. I get it I understand, I do not know what I would have done in this situation me having taken care of children myself. When you are dealing with children it can be difficult. The decisions you must make are difficult because although your emotions say one thing, you must make the rational and responsible decision. This is not always the easy, but it is the way things need to be handled at times.)

Life went on and continued, I had now been in high school for 2 years. It seemed as though the only light I had was my nephew. Thankfully, my sister needed lots of help with my nephew. Her and my mother were very close, I got to spend lots of time with him. Looking back at things now I am so thankful for this because it was him that gave me hope, hope for happiness me seeing and feeling his unconditional love. I was trying to discover what I was supposed to do and who I was supposed to be, after I got out of high school. I went to my guidance counselor who apologized for putting me in the hospital explaining she did not have a choice. I knew though never to trust her with my true feelings after that day. I had been trained from the beginning of my life though how to lie to the "people at school" as my mom called them. I never told her too much after that, but we did discuses my future. She mentioned she remembered how much I loved my nephew. She suggested I try out the early childhood education program as an elective at the school. There was a preschool inside the school where the kids, from two to five years old, attended half a day and we got to interact with the kids as part of our assignment. As I interacted with the kids, I knew right away that this was something I really enjoyed doing. I decided, this is what I was going to do. I pursued it and decided to get my teaching license to teach preschool children. As part of my assignment in getting my license I had to work a specific number of hours with children. I was led to get a job at the YMCA for afterschool care. This is the start of my new beginning, where God used one person to help change the rest of life.

# CHAPTER 6

# PIECES OF LIGHT INTO DARKNESS

$\mathcal{O}$n this path of finding who I was, I realized my love for children. I found a job working at the YMCA in an elementary school with school age children. I loved it! the kids were so much fun. For the first time I felt as I was making a difference. There working at the YMCA I had to go through a training process, I was put with a group leader Mary. The kids just loved her, she was very meek, quiet, and sweet. She was incredibly good with the kids in keeping them in line as well as having such a good time. As time went on Mary and I became awfully close. Working together side by side every day. I also got to know my other coworkers well but not as close as I was with Mary. I at times spent time with her after work or she would give me rides home from work. She began to know and see my struggles as she got to know me.

I felt safe to confided in Mary, she was the gentle and sweet person. That sweet softness that you are supposed to get from your mom, I got it from her. I loved that about her, no one in my life was like her. Mary meant a lot at this point in my life. I began to pour out all my struggles to her. It was easy to do, as she was an incredibly good listener. I needed this very much in my life as I struggled with depression and loneliness. I began to pour my heart out to her; I told her things that I never told anyone else. Such as, I told her I tried to commit suicide at fifteen. Even though I knew God, knew what it would mean if I had gone through with it. She then began to get concerned and emphasized on me going to church. She talked to me about God, asking if I had ever asked him into my life. I told her, I had prayed and asked God into my heart when I was a kid, so I thought I was ok.

Because of my home life and the struggles that were constant day to day, I decided I was going to get two jobs. I was going to get out. I could not live in that so-called hell anymore. So, I came up with a plan. I would have two jobs and I would move out and live on my own. And then, I would be happy.

I somehow talked my mom into helping me do so. She was able to help get the "f\*\*\* out", as she would say. However, this would only happen on or after my eighteenth birthday.

We found a small place close by, it was small.

It was privately owned, I needed to have a dog for protection. I was going to bring my dog Princess, a big Labrador. The landlord was not very happy about the dog but agreed signing a lease.

It was all set. My eighteenth birthday was on a weekend, and I was all set to move out. I thought my life was going to change. I had spoken to all my coworkers and had asked for their help.

I had it all planned and ready. That Friday, on my birthday, I was so excited. Then, I got a phone call on my cell phone at work. I asked my boss if I could answer it and with permission, I did.

My job was in a school, so I went into the hallway. My coworkers and myself were all in one room and the games for the kids were in the cafeteria. To be alone, I had to go into the hallway. It was the landlord of the apartment I was supposed to be renting and moving into that day. The conversation went from me being excited to talk to him to me being terribly upset by the end of the conversation. Apparently, the landlord had found someone else to rent the apartment. Some one that did not have a dog and he was happier with renting the place to them. At this point, I had searched for weeks trying to find this place. This place had been my last option, I hung up the phone. I walked back into the cafeteria. I looked over on the other side of the room. There Mary was standing with a smile on her face, looking at me. She could see on my face that something was wrong. I remember it like a movie. Her slowly walking towards me. Her finally getting to me and asking what was wrong. I explained to her what happened. As I did, I had an uncontrollable number of tears pouring down my face. She said, "it will be alright", "tomorrow would be better".

Then she got the kids to sing and dance around the table where I was sitting. When the kids went back to play, Mary and I talked some more. Although we could not fully discuss everything because we were at work. She looked at me and again said "It will be ok. Tomorrow will be better". She continued, saying "Today is your birthday. I will come over and we'll have a good time". I then looked at her and said "Yeah tomorrow, will be better because I will not be here". She knew exactly what I had meant because I had already spoken to her about my past. She looked at me and that meek, quiet girl changed into a very firm face and voice. With a very stern voice, she looked at me and said "No, tomorrow will be better because you will be here." She told me she would come over and have cake with me. That had been the plan, anyways.

We finished off the workday and headed to my house. As soon as we walked into the door, my mother had heard from the landlord. She blamed me and was screaming and cursing like no other. The very thing I wanted to get away from.

Mary and I went into my room and closed the door to drown out the sound of my mother screaming. We sat and talked as I bawled my eyes out. I continued to tell her, "I don't not want to live anymore". She asked, "I know you've gone to church before, but when was the last time you asked Jesus into your heart?" I said, "when I was kid". She said "I think you need to do it again. And He'll come in and fix this brokenness inside of you."

We talked for quite some time. I got saved that night, on my birthday Oct 3, 2006.

Just before she left, she told me I could start going to church with her and she would start picking me up for church. I had grown up knowing who God was because of my grandfather, also as I said my mom tried. We went sometimes even when we first moved to Tampa. We were involved in a church where I worked as the Sunday school teacher. It was a small church, the pastors even then saw the call of my life with children. As far as my understanding of God, I cannot say I still understood a whole lot about God although that Pastors were great, I do not remember my understanding of God ever really growing I was also incredibly young and went, when my mother felt like going. At this point going to church with Mary was easy because I had been. Although it was still a new place so, I cannot say I was not nervus. The fact that it was with her made it easier for sure though. I went on a Wednesday night. I remember walking in and feeling a love that I had never felt before. I felt a presence that I had never felt before. A part of me wanted to run away. I felt undeserving because my whole life I was told I was worth nothing. Also, the New York came out in me as well, in a way the people where I want used to in New York it is not normal for people to be so loving and nice. At this church, all these people were coming up to me and being so loving and kind that it was weirding me out. Honestly, it was more about the family dynamic I grew up with. It was not normal for me, the positivity coming from the congregation. I remember that night so well. All I kept thinking was I want to run. I wanted out, but I had no way to get home.

I drove with Mary; the church was meeting at a hotel. I walked out of the room where we were because of that feeling of needing to run. I walked down the hallway there was a door at the end of a hallway with a window I stared up at the moon. Remember thinking, I wanted was to be at my favorite place, a pier. This was a park not too far from my house this was my place the only place I found peace. I turned around and there was Mary. She asked, "what was wrong?" I said I wanted to run and want to leave". She looked at me and said "uh uh, come on let's go. We are going back into the service. You need this." We then went back into the service and again as I walked through the door, I felt that same presence all over again. I remember that the whole time as I was sitting, I felt that presence. Now I know that it was God, His presence filled that room. At the end of the service, there was an altar call. I felt a tug on my heart. I did not know what it was, so I raise my hand said the sinner's prayer. I met a few people after, that were nice. That night was just the beginning of the rest of my life changing.

# CHAPTER 7

# PIECES OF TRANSFORMATION

*A*s time went on, I continued to attend church with Mary. Slowly with this new friendship I found with Mary, but most of all Jesus. Things began to change; I began building relationships with others at the church. I attended classes; at the time I believe it was called new Christianity 101 series went on to 201 etc. This was all good because I began for the first time in my life started building friendships that felt more like family. I began learning what healthy relationships were and what it was like to feel and be loved for the first time. Well let's just say because I grew up in such a broken unhealthy environment, I was a crazy teen. With no real understanding of what were healthy boundaries. To be honest I really did not know boundaries at all. It was a hard road a head although things were getting better, there still was a lot of work in me that needed to be done. I was somehow I was still excepted by people in church. Well, by most let's just leave it at that. I had and still have a very loud personality, not everyone was very fond of this. Just imagine a loud, speaking her mind, New York state of mind teen with no boundaries, that came from a very chaotic home, although a girl who had the biggest heart there ever was. Yup, that was me. To say the very least there still was a lot of work to be done in me, but there were a few people there who still loved and accepted me. It felt amazing, to be a part of something that was not full of chaos and dysfunction. I always knew I wanted to be different but did not always know how. There is one couple that accepted me and loved me right from the start Jen & Sam Bermudez. Who I still might I add are a part of my family today. They have two children, there son Gio who was about 3 years old. Bella, Jen was pregnant with. They are from up north too Jersey and Philly also being Hispanic they understood my crazy. I loved that they just loved me. They became the youth leaders and I then got to spend a lot of time with them. We had so many youth events from carwashes to raise money for upcoming events, fun sporting events, youth lock-ins (where you stayed overnight in church played fun games) and youth worship night so much more. It was Just what I needed, Although I was still working through the feelings of depression and suicidal thoughts the fact that I had this new family it was not so lonely as it used to be. Although I still remember often driving home with Mary dropping me off, the feeling of not just wanting to go home.

The school year my final year of high school was also coming to an end. I was at this point on OJT (On the Job training) for the rest of the school year. I worked at the YMCA on some mornings then it was home after during school hours. Then it was

80

back to the Y at 2 till 6pm. It was a little bit lonely at this point because the only place I had to escape was the Y. I loved not having to get up super early, to catch the bus. I still had to get up early some mornings to work but it was not every morning, so it wasn't so bad. Having to spend more time at home was not as fun ether. Because of the constant yelling, if my mother was not yelling about one thing, it was another she would say, "You need to get up and clean do something! because you're not going to sit on your Fat a** and do nothing all day".

I was also enrolled in night classes to obtain my license to teach preschool children. It was my senior year of high school so that when all was said and done when the year was over, I would be able to go right into teaching preschool. The classes were only two nights a week it was a break yet, I still had to endure the rest of the time at home, when I did not have church or work. In Oldsmar there is a park called R.E Old s Park. It is right on the bay, with a long pier. I would ride my bike there often when things would get bad day or night, it became my place of escape. I would go and pray, listen to music, and spend time with God. (Still till this day it has become one of my favorite places).

Although it was hard to deal with the way my mother treated me, I started to respond differently to my mother's outburst and abusive behavior. As I began to learn who God was and what the word of God says about honoring your parents (Mind you I was not perfect) I began to change. She started to notice I remember her yelling and saying, "what are those people doing to you?" She could not believe how much I had started to change and when God had started to change in me. I invited her to church, and she agreed I still remember her saying "I gotta go meet these people". My mother agreeing to go to church was the start of change. I remember this day so clearly. She went up to the alter, wept and she got prayed for. I had already been at the church with Mary for about 4 or 5 months. Things began to change at home. She did not go to church every Sunday, but she did begin to go.

As the year began to come to an end my grandfather passed away. I was super sad being that he was the only believer in Christ in our family I never got to tell him about my new church and newfound deep foundation of faith. We all as A family piled up in my mom's car and drove to New York to his funeral. Shortly after coming back, we moved to a house my uncle bought in Tampa far, far from Oldsmar. About an hour's drive on a good day 45 mins. So far, one of My best friends now her husband and my good friend Brian wrote a song about it "Esther". Brain and I also worked at the YMCA together from time to time. He became a close friend and like a brother always making me and anyone around him laugh. His twin brother Brock also worked with us. So, fun! Two lifelong friends. Although we do not see each other often I will always consider them to be like brothers and great friends.

I than had my H.S Graduation 2006 also the completion of my class to be a licensed preschool teacher. To celebrate me graduating high school and receiving my teaching license to teach. My mother threw me a party for me, I invited all the people I had grown close to at church just about all the youth leaders and also the pastors. With My mom coming to church when she could she had also made a good friend who had come as well, it was such a great day. I remember feeling so loved and supported. Then a few weeks later was my graduation. My mother, grandmother, sister, nephew came along with Mary.

Shortly after graduation I found my first teaching job as a preschool teacher. Little Ones preschool it has now since closed. It was where my journey with children started. I had a 4-year-old VPK class. I was very enthusiastic, excited about the job but also very scared. I honestly had no idea what I was doing up until this point, other than doing the classes and taking care of after school children. I really had not taught a class before. I am so grateful and thankful that I had such an amazing, amazing boss and director that just poured into me so much knowledge and helped me along, she was one of the sweetest women I had ever meet. This preschool was a part of a church, all the teachers were so great. I was the youngest lead teacher and was embraced by all these amazing women. I was also able to teach and talk about God which was also great. Still to this day I am so thankful for that first year. It was sometimes challenging and scary the not knowing. Having such an amazing gentle, loving and God-fearing boss to help guide me, as well as to put me in my place when I needed it. One of my favorite memories about being there was on my lunch breaks I was able to just freely worship making up my own songs on a grand piano belonging to the church and I was allowed to play. I just remember sitting thinking of the future and praying. Work had now become my escape, the feeling I had knowing the difference I was making in each of those kids lives felt amazing. It had given me purpose. Yet with all this new Joy, things really started to get crazy at home. With my grandfather passing my mother had been given a lot of inheritance. Unfortunately, with money comes temptation. She was at her best health wise but got involved with the wrong people. When you have lots of money people tend to show up. I guess. she made the choice to use again, she relapsed. Let's just say things at home were not pleasant at all. As the year came to an end I was unfortunately laid off, nothing I did, just me being the new girl. There was low state founding for the preschool and the number of children being low. I was so devastated, yet I understood.

I went on the search for a new job as soon as I found one another preschool. I then decided to leave getting a place of my own. I just could not be in that environment anymore. I was also traveling so far to church twice a week or more and being that all my friends lived in the area as well. It just made sense, it had always been my goal to move out and be on my own. Create a nice peaceful home for myself. So, I did, I moved to Clearwater, Fl. I got a one bed one bath a place, it was one of the biggest steps I was finally able to make. I also began to get counseling from the pastor's wife. This was where so many things that were uncovered during our sessions. It was then I began learning so much about who I was in Christ, how much I was loved by him. I remember so vividly the first session what I was wearing a long sleeve blue shirt (it is crazy the details you remember from such a vital part of life). I broke down so many times during this session. She started the session by, asking me about my childhood, we started from the very beginning. As I went through each stage of my life telling the stories, she would stop me uncovering where in life things like rejection and fear began to rule over my life. This went on for quite some time three to four session later I had learned so much about myself. As she did this, we would stop each time and pray over each thing that was uncovered. There was so much to be done. I had gone through so much it was going to take more than just a few sessions with her. She did not always have the time being a pastor's wife. I had been going to the youth group and begin to grow closer to two of the other youth leaders James and Phillis Harden and just like Jen and Sam excepted and loved me brokenness and all. showing so much love and compassion. My counseling sessions were continued with them, I would go to their house some nights, or they would even travel to mine which for them was extremely far, they had two young children of their own. They showed such tremendous sacrifice for me. They were led by the Holy Spirit and would not leave of stop the session unless they felt it was time to. Some sessions where hours long uncovering, praying, and spending time just loving me. Still to this day I say there is nothing like a Phyllis hug! You can just feel the love in every embrace. I forgot to mention James, worked late most of these nights and still showed up, still listened. He may or may not dosed off here and there I do not blame him with was mostly when I would go off on a tangent. Anyone who knows me, knows I can talk and talk…. Blab when sleepy. They were such a vital part of who I have become today. I mean think of how blessed I am to have had hours and hours of free counseling. During these hours I began to learn so much about myself and who I was, who I wanted to be and how so many things I had felt about who I was where lies. I began to find a deeper meaning to life, who I was becoming. What I

ME

wanted to become, then began realizing I had worth. Just the feeling of knowing how much so many loved me was the most amazing feeling I had ever felt. As I began to learn more and more of God's word and all he had for me I began to believe and hold on to one of my favorite Bible verse, still to this day.

> "For I know the plans I have for you," declares the LORD, "plans to prosper you and not to harm you, plans to give you hope and a future" Jeramiah 29:11 NIV

Truly those words, every word became so real to me. The person I was, the hurt I had gone although. I really began to believe God's truth he, was and would turn my destiny around. I would and could have a different and better life. Although this change and hope came into my life, believe me, there was not happy roses and butterflies. This was and will continue to be a constant choice. As time went on, my relationship with Phillis and James grew as I continued counseling with them. This was also in many ways as it was good, and it was a scary time in my life. Although I was going through this amazing life change. Loneliness started to creep in once again yes, I still had to deal with this. I was living alone for the first time although I had and was still undergoing so many great life changes. The one very thing I had been so happy about living on my own, I was away from the chaos that I was constantly surrounded with. In this new season of my life was much more peaceful and I began the healing of my past. For the first time in my life, I really was alone. The realization of that at times became overwhelming, this was when I really needed God more than ever. Because I had learned with him, I was never alone. I am a people person and because I was alone so much of my childhood, this was a struggle. Sometimes daily I had to lean on God. I did have a hard time with it, at times, yes. I am not going to tell any lies. I sometimes would give in to loneliness, I was still learning. Let's face it, I am human these are things sometimes in life that are going to come against us when the enemy whispers in our ear. It is our choice to give into those feelings or not. I found it to be such a struggle when I felt lonely, sometimes to even go to God in prayer and trust Him. Let me tell you, though I learned quickly when I did that it really is not and was not that hard at all. God's love for us is so gentle and loving. Literally at times the burden of loneliness just melted away when I cried out to Him. God takes our burdens when we ask. Sometimes it's just that simple. On the other side of that, sometimes are harder than others we just must learn to trust Him. As I began trusting him more and more in this time of my life, I began to enjoy life more. I got more involved in my church and continued hours of counseling; I began to see a change. I began making even more friends that have now become lifelong friends more life family.

This was the time in my life I met Madi. I was so crazy, silly, and outgoing but she just loved me, we hit it off and started spending a lot of time together. I still remember the first time we had a sleepover we barely knew one another and yup that was me "Hey want to come spend the night lol" she was crazy enough to do it still to this day I just remember the fun and laughter we had that night.

Madi was still living at home with her parents, she was 17 when we met. (I am older lol 6 months older) her parents also went to the church, and I had met them there. I was known as Crazy loud Esther. Mark and Cindy did not care that I was loud or crazy they too had just welcomed and loved me as Madi did. As time went on, Madi and I became best friends and spent a lot of time together. I also became really close with both her parents. I just could not get over how and why in all my brokenness and mess that I was, how all these amazing things just began happening. I know now God brought all these amazing people that I so needed in my life. Them accepting me as I was, that was big. As God began to heal me, he began use all these people in my life that you will hear though out my story to help me mature and grow. There were a lot of hard lessons I had to learn over the years. Through the loving care of those who were around me, that became family to me. I learned those lessons with their help. I was not always the easiest person to deal with, there was a lot of work to do. From the lack of so much in my childhood years. What was amazing was I begun to see and feel what it was like to have people in my life that were not going to walk away when things got hard. Seeing and knowing what this felt like, it made me want to change. As I continued counseling with James and Phillis, I really began to become like a sponge trying so hard to change, letting things of my past go and trying my best to become a different person. Different from what I knew to be normal. As I continued going to the youth group, I began building more and more friendships. I then met Audra. Audra and I began getting close. We just clicked both being from New York also having the same taste in music as well as the same kind of humor. It was still extremely hard for me to trust, although I had made lots of new friends, I only had a few I could and really did trust. For the next few years Madi and Audra where my people. We did so much together, as a group or with the youth group and me with one or the other. Although I spent time with others and had other friendships, these became my girls. The year of living alone abruptly came to an end. When my car just died and there was no coming back. Because if this I no longer could afford to live on my own because I had to get a new car and was barely making enough to make it on my own. I had kept in touch with my family. Although at a distance it was just so hard to see and watch the chaos.

Now it was time that I had to move back in with my mom. She had still been attending the church and we would try and spend time together when we could. It wasn't always bad, I had some of my guy friends help me move Mom lived in New Port Richey where she was renting a house. At the time I had been working in a preschool in Clearwater, so it was not that long of a drive. I eventually got another car after moving, I was also helping her rent and what I could. Living with her, this time was not always easy, yet barrable in my ways being that I had, had a life now and a job to go to. I kept busy while living there, it was not too bad. As we also started going to counseling with the pastor's wife. The most amazing thing began to happen, my mother started changing, listening to what she was told to do in counseling. It was crazy, like I was seeing a whole new person. She listened to how I felt and listened to the counselor which was Extremely BIG. I had never in my life seen or heard my mother change or listen to anyone EVER. She was

Extremely independent. As far as advice goes, she took what she liked normally and threw what she did not like away. We were at such a good place, So, much so I wanted to do something nice for her.

I planned a surprise birthday party for her. I invited all our close friends and created a video about how much I loved her and appreciated her. The party turned out great and she said she really loved everything, and she was very thankful.

After a year of living there together we had to move. We moved closer to the church and work which was nice, we moved to Dunedin. It was in an apartment complex, I loved living there, there was a pool. We also now lived so close to the beach. Things where so great us living together, it was not so bad. But now that we had a pool my sister and uncle visited more. It was great until someone my mother was introduced to; he was one of my uncle's friends. Then things really started to change. My Mothers cancer had been in remission. She was at an incredibly good place and so was our relationship. Again, I would say not perfect we had our ups and downs, but things were better. That all began to change shortly after moving to this new place. After meeting my uncle's friend let's call him "Joe". She Began dating him, shortly soon thereafter he moved in with us. From the very beginning he and I truly did not see eye to eye. I saw right through him and knew all he wanted to do was take advantage of my mother. She did not see it; she just saw him and the fact that she was not alone. I was still working and help paying rent. He moved in and paid nothing. I was terribly upset by this; my mother really did not need my help but made me pay for rent and bills. But I was obedient and just continued,

Joe was not a Christian at all, he was very nasty to me. My relationship with my mom started to fall apart, things went from us fixing things slowly healing our relationship. To us not talking much, arguing daily and not spending time with one another.

# CHAPTER 8

# SURVIVING PIECES OF A BROKEN HEART

*I* continued to go to church and being around my friends and church family once again became my only outlet. I began hanging more and more with Audra. We began spending a lot of time together we became inseparable. I began to also spend a lot of time with her parents. They became the family I always wanted and needed; I began spending Sundays after church at their house. Sunday was the best, they are Italian, so Sunday was meatball and pasta day! Boy was there always a spread; Audra's dad Uncle Leo was and is still an amazing cook. So was Aunt Mary Lou, but her area in the kitchen was and is baking. She makes the BEST chocolate chip cookies. Over the years I have learned so much from Uncle Leo, he has given me a lot of yummy cooking recipes and ways of cooking. I also began spending all my holidays with them as well. It was so amazing to see a family even in their imperfections love one another, having such a great and good healthy time. I had not ever known what this was like. So many relationships and sweet memories with this family I will forever cherish. To name few sweet, sweet Papa! Papa lives with uncle Leo and Aunt Mary Lou. One of the sharpest older men I have ever known, also the wittiest always telling jokes and old war stories. Has the biggest heart of them all. Then there was Uncle Leo's brother who has now gone to be with the Lord, Uncle Lieco. He was a big-hearted goof! It was so fun watch the relationship between him and his brother uncle Leo. They both loved cooking. We would all play family a games and let's just say they were both very competitive. Alongside Uncle Lieco was his son who I also love so much Paul. Paul I also knew from church as he was one of the youth leaders. He is like a big brother to me. Although I know I drove him crazy at times. He became my chiropractor and then my boss. I worked for him in his chiropractic office. I did different projects he had me do, cleaning organizing files etc. Let's just say, he loved me even then when I was a bit crazy to say the least. I never, I mean never, worked in a professional setting. He loved me despite some mistakes young Esther had to learn, here is a quick story to give you all an example I was about 19, he asked me to watch the front desk, so I did. Someone had come in to see him. I called him to the front office. As he was talking to the person, I was behind him in a chair with a big ol lollypop in my mouth. Spinning like a little child in the office chair, while waiting for my next assignment. Sooo not professional, let's just say we had a talk, and I never did that again. But despite that he still loved me, forgave me with the promise of never doing that again. So many more relatives to speak of that loved me. I love and am grateful for each one.

In this season of my life, I learned so much about Gods love for me, and just how and why He brought all these amazing people into my life when I needed it the most. I had never known or seen a family that knew how to function and love one another since the small glimpse I got with Ms. Johnson's family years before. Especially with what was happening with my relationship with my mother that was falling apart again.

As things were still falling apart at home, I made a ridiculously huge, scary mistake. I was driving and I looked down for a CD that had fallen in my car. I looked up the next moment I was crashing into a car. I totaled my car smashing the front completely, thank God I was not hurt nor was anyone else. I had insurance, but I did not have money saved, I was left with no car and no money for a down payment for a new one. So, I went to my mother asking for help despite the way things were with us. She gave me money to put as a down payment, saying "I will give you the money to you because, I'm not going to drive you to work" But I want my money back". I told her I would pay her back. Not knowing she wanted it back right way, on top of me paying her rent. I thought I had time, after only a couple of weeks of her lending me the money she said, "I need my money". I told her "I did not have it"; I was just a preschool teacher not making much money. But I would try my best, she then gave me a deadline I could not fulfill. Saying, "If I don't see my money by the end of the week, I'm going to put your sh*** out on the street". I was being kicked out. What hurt more in all of this, more than her kicking me out. Was that she had this man who was not working and helping with anything. I was helping best I could, and she was kicking me out knowing I had nowhere to go, choosing him over me. This completely devastated me. I had met a newer friend Beth at church, I mentioned my situation to her she said, "I have an extra room and you can come live with me". Once again God had provided and made a way. My heart broken; my mother would do that to me. I would forgive her; we would fix things. Healing our relationship like putting a band-aid over it, with wounds still untouched underneath. In times like this, it felt like she just ripped that band-aid right off. It was so painful, yet it was something out of my control.

I was so grateful for this new friend who had offered and now given me a place to live. Within the week I moved in with her, things where great, so peaceful she was always smiling, was just so happy and encouraging. This lasted a few weeks as I attempted to get on my feet, trying to find a second job so that I could move out on my own. I saw this as a temporary place, but she had told me there was no rush in moving. Then she gave me the news she was moving, I had about a month to find somewhere else to live. As grateful as I was for her giving me a place to live, I was devastated because I had no place to go and still did not make enough money to live on my own. But I had to figure something else out, I was now on the hunt for a home. I remember talking to Audra just crying my eyes out saying, I did not know what to do or how I was going to do it. It was than she suggested to talk to her dad, Uncle Leo. About a bought that, she told me how he had helped her, teaching her how to bouget. The next day, I called him told him what was going on and if he could help me in any way. We met and came up with what I could afford per month, now that I had a better idea of what I could pay per month. I had some home-work to do in finding a place. After my search Uncle Leo said come back and we will see what your options are, together. A week or two later, after doing research on so places, Audra and I went on the search for a new place for me to call home. Unfortunately, the places that were within my budget, were not in the best of areas. This made things hard with me being alone. The last thing I wanted to do was live in an unsafe area. During our search we passed a hotel, where we both knew the manger, from church and I also had nannied for him and his wife. Audra and I looked at each other and said jokingly "we should see if I can live there". We both laughed it off and kept driving it was probably the only laughter of the day. By the end of the day, I remember feeling hopeless, saddened by the choices of unsafe potential homes. The day ended Audra and I saw the last option and we headed back to her house to report back to Uncle Leo what we had found. He was just as unhappy about what we had found as I was. After seeing the disappointment on his face for me. I wanted to lighten things up as I often do. I told him about how we had passed the hotel saying, "yeah living there would be much better than most of the places we had seen". I began laughing. It was then like a light went off in his head, he looked at me saying,

"What is so funny about that?! That is a great idea, for some-thing temporary it cannot hurt to ask. Since you know the manger, he may want to help being he knows and cares about you. You should call him; you are running out of time before you must find a place".

The next day I called the manger, I told him what happened. He then said "I would love to help because me and my wife love you. But he would have to get back to me". I called and told Uncle Leo. He told me to wait and see what the hotel manager came back with. Uncle Leo then told me call him when I heard back, and we would again together make the decision together. A few days later I got a phone call from the manger for a very reasonably workable amount he could allow me to live at the hotel temporarily. I then called Uncle Leo, we made the decision, that this was what was best thing for me right now. About a week later I moved in, it was just a simple room with a bathroom. I was grateful beyond words; I remember being so happy knowing I would have a safe place. Although I was incredibly grateful to have a good safe roof over my head, the thought of the situation I was in weighed on me. After getting settled in, I remember this night like it was yesterday. I just fell to my knees loudly I began sobbing. Crying out to God asking "Why?!!? I have been so faithful in trying to do what was right, I have gone to church served in the church. My life I said was supposed to be getting better now, that I knew and serve you God". I sobbed for hours that night until falling asleep, I wish I could say that was the last time I cried myself to sleep in that hotel room. It was not, I began dealing with a heavy weight of depression once again. I did what I believe, I should always do when under the strong attack of the enemy, when he is using depressing and oppression against me. Although there was a very real sad reality that I was facing I had to make a choice, I began to listen to worship music in those moments alone crying and as bad as I felt. I knew, just knew God was going to change things and make a way. I knew, I needed God more than ever. Did I cry yes, did I feel sad yes, did loneliness get to me yes. Did thoughts of worthlessness come yes, but I pushed back saying to myself how loved I was. I remined myself although it was sad living in a hotel, but just how much of a blessing it was to have a good safe place to rest my head. I would cry feeling the feelings of depression and loneliness. Crying myself to sleep many nights, underneath all that I still believed God would make a way. At the end of the night, I remember many times feeling and knowing God was with me. Uncle Leo and Aunt Mary Lou were very present and supportive in this time of searching for a safe place as the hotel was just another temporary home. They both knew my struggle emotionally. I was open and honest with them; they would always tell me to just trust God. A month after living at the hotel, Uncle Leo and Aunt Mary Lou called asking if I would come over to their house, because they had some-thing to talk with me, telling me had something they wanted to tell me. This day was that day everything changed for me. They told me God had put on their hearts to bless me and give me a good, healthy, and safe place to live. They wanted to bless me buying a condo. In a good safe area, I remember tears of all kinds from many different emotions at once filling my eyes. In disbelief saying "really?! really?!!" And smiles planted on both their faces. Aunt Mary Lou saying "Yes we Love you Esther, we want you to be in a good safe place to call home, it's just going to take a little while. We will take you to see some places." I then thanked them hugging and kissing them. (Sometimes we can get stuck on or blinded by what is in front of us. The realness of the things in our lives. It may seem impossible to believe and have faith that God is working. You may think that all is lost. The truth is, when we trust God, no matter what is happening in our lives, God is always working on something bigger and better. Also, God says if you are faithful in Him, the enemy will have to give back what he stole seven times over)

In Proverbs 6:31 KJV it says, "But if he be found, he shall restore sevenfold; he shall give all the substance of his house".

After a few months I then got a phone call that some of the condos I could potentially live in were ready to look at. Uncle Leo and Aunt Mary Lou asked me to come look at some with them. I remember being so excited to see these potential homes. Thinking I may have a place of my own to call home. So that afternoon we went out looking. Although I was grateful for just about anything, I was so excited to be part of the process. All the places were great but there were two that I had my eye on. I was not pushy yet very respectful letting them know which ones I really liked and had my eye on.

# CHAPTER 9

# PIECES OF RESTORED HOPE

*T*he day ended, I could not have felt more grateful and happy. I went back and began making plans on just what colors I wanted my new home to be and how I wanted it to look. I also came up with a budget on how much I could spend and began getting some of the things to help make my home, mine. Before I knew it after living in the hotel for almost 6 months, I got the call from Uncle Leo that one of the condos I had chosen and really loved would be ready soon, he would call me letting me know when I would be able to move in. I was extremally excited.

I cannot say that I am most coordinated person, so clumsy I trip over my own feet kind of person. I was going to church one night leaving the hotel, do not ask me how, but I somehow missed a step in the hotel and fell down a few feet of steps. Twisting my ankle badly, I was taken to the hospital in an ambulance. It was truly more embarrassing then hurtful. Here I was on the middle of the lobby floor now hurt, in the place that was giving me a break to begin with. I was still working as a pre-school teacher, and I was thankful my bosses worked with me during this time. The next day after falling Uncle Leo called saying that the condo was ready, he had a key and wanted to sit down and talk and give me a key. He knew I had fallen, asked if I wanted to wait. I of course told him no, that I would get help. I asked a few friends and they offered to help. Unfortunately, not until that weekend it was the middle of the week. So, what do I do? being it was the middle of the week, I could not wait I began moving things in, hopping up the stairs. Smart right? No but I was so overjoyed I did not care I could not wait. After hopping bringing a few things, I eventually made it to the weekend. All my friends came moving me into the condo and out of the hotel. It was great close to work and church. This was such a huge blessing with all that I had been though all I ever wanted was a place to call home and thanks to God putting it in Uncle Leo and Aunt Mary Lou's hearts, I now had one. They were very gracious to me with rent until I got on my feet, I knew I needed to get a seconded job. I had heard of an online nanny service and signed up. I had already done some side on call work, through a nanny agency for date night nanny jobs. Like when I worked for done hotel manager and his wife. I thought, why not trying to work for a family as a nanny, for my secondary job. Trying this website, I had never done it this way before just over the internet. To be honest it was a little scary, So I decided to ask Aunt Mary Lou to come with me on interviews staying in the car. I went on many interviews, but one I just knew was a fit. I was hired. Little did I know it would forever change my life in more ways than one.

I got hired to work for the Hauk family. Mom Karen, Father Earl, children Madison and Tyler. The kids were four and six, from one of the very first days with them it was just so fun. We bonded almost instantly as they took to my silly and fun personality with a balance of discipline of course. It was such a joy watching them grow, coming up with new fun activities to do daily and on rainy days watching movies that became staples in our relationship. The Madea movies were a favorite, being that the kids were of course a little older. Right from the start as I began to build a relationship with (Mom and Dad) Karen and Earl I was accepted and so appreciated for all I did. As time went on, I then became like family because they knew my upbringing and family life was like for me even more, so they just took me in lovingly building traditions with the kids like me staying overnight every Christmas eve to wake up and have Christmas morning with them. I became like another one of their children. Karen and I, over the years' time had just got closer with time. During this time, I was still attending the same church still counseling and doing lots of different things in and for church so I can say it was a busy time. Things would still happen, and I just had to deal with them in time of my life a little differently. I was trying to find this new happy and healing, I at times had to separate myself from the negative. That meant anyone or anything that just was not good for me. I had a decision after somethings happened with my father. I made the decision to let him go for a while. When I was done healing in other areas I would re- address the relationship. In this time, I had two jobs working for the preschool mornings then the Hauk family in the afternoon twelve-hour days. I loved it, I still had many ups and downs emotionally none the less I was healing. For the most part this was a really good time in my life, until trouble came when I had to find a new job at a preschool because where I was the preschool had to lay me off. I was really blessed knowing the Hauk's who had so many friends that had young kids. For short times here and there. Different friends of the Hauk family used me as their nanny to help me until I got on my feet. One my favorite families, with two of my favorite people Rod and Jen. The B family still to this day like an aunt and uncle, I love them. They have four kids Josh, Jacob, Jaden and Jenna. During the time of my being laid off, it just so happened to be that their nanny would be out for a few weeks. I took over for her, while searching for a new job. The youngest the girls were so little and fun. The two boys were just as fun!

Another family I became close with was the Q family they also lived in the neighborhood. Madison who I already took care of everyday, was best friends with the Q family's youngest daughter Mia. I would often babysit Mia. Mia was the fun yet sassy little one, with the biggest heart. I also became great friends with the Q parents who also are such great people. Mia's mom Lainie Has become one of my close friends. I also worked for a few other families that were friends of the Hauk's, that also lived in neighborhood on a as needed basis. I built so many wonderful lifelong friendships in just this one neighborhood. I could not be more thankful. Because all the families lived in the same neighborhood as the Hauk family that I worked for the next 6 years. I never loss touch or went without seeing all of the other kids I helped care for in the neighborhood. I went to all the kid's events for holidays, birthdays etc. that the parents hosted.

After my time ended with the B family when their nanny returned. I started full-time at a new preschool. This next pre-school was a real test, of my faith, I had no idea what was coming to say it nicely. This became a rough road for me daily, she was very nice to me in the beginning of me working there. Then, like a light switch she suddenly changed. She began treating me terribly. Not just me, I also noticed her treating the other staff and even children terribly. The other teachers had tried to warn me she would change. They said, she could be good one day/week or even two, then she would change and not be as nice. It was like it was literally like dealing with a person with two personalities. She did not have the same belief system. She knew what my beliefs where and she was not a fan of them. Boy, did the enemy use her. It felt as though I became a target for all her anger and things she was dealing with, she took it out on me. The school was not very big, there was only two other teachers. One of them I truly know God knew what he was doing having her there. She is a believer, she helped me daily. I call her my real Life Madea, she just kept a smile on my face even on the hardest of days.

This woman we worked for just was not right, she had a lot of issues. I stayed of course, the time I did because I loved the children because I did love my job.

I stared to journal every morning, I would come in and some-times she was nice and oh so sweet and then other times she was just downright nasty ready to pick a fight over just about anything. After being at the school for about six months, it was being shut down. Because this director was not following rules and not doing things right financially. At the time I did not know what I was going to do next. I remember talking to the mom of the Q family, Lanie. She told me there was an opening working for an office job. With her. She would talk to her boss getting me an interview. So, I did in the week before the schools closing and yet again God saved me getting me in with this new office position working for HCA. I had not really worked in an office much before, other than when I had with Paul in his chiropractic office.

During the interview I was told, I would be trained. I go the job, it turned out to be perfect because I could go in the hours, I needed then leave in time to take care of the Hauk children. This job was great experience in learning professionalism as I worked with women who were older than me and all taught me different things. The woman I had to work with sided by side was so sweet, Fran was her name, she along with Lanie helped me learn all I needed to learn to do my job successfully. Also, my Boss Woah talk about night and day difference from the previous boss, in how amazing she was to me. Sue, one of the most understanding, caring and Loving bosses I have had. Working here was simply great in many ways.

After some time, about a year or so, this new job had become mundane, it wasn't fulfilling. My heart has always been to work with children. Although I was still working for the Hauk family as the kids go older, I was needed less. Until I began to clean once a week and no longer care for the children. Being in this environment working with ladies every day, we each had our own jobs and we all most times stayed to ourselves getting our work done. I began to just feel so lonely, as much as I appreciated my job, I lived alone, and loneliness began to set in. In this time of loneliness, I thought I would find "Happily ever after" I began a relationship over the phone mostly me being hopeful. Thinking it would go somewhere eventually. I started talking to John. Shortly after beginning this relationship, I got a devastating news that my aunt my mother's sister had passed away. This was my favorite aunt; I was so saddened by this news myself and mother both dropped everything and of course attended the funeral in New York. During this time, I had just started taking to this John we talked the whole time during this trip. At the time as sad as I was it was nice to have someone to talk to. This trip to New York with my mom the first trip back to New York, with her as an adult was just a roller coaster. One minute we were fine and the next we were fighting. It was a very intense trip with both of our emotions running extremely high, with the death of my aunt. It was nice to have John to talk to and bounce things off, we had this connection. He just knew how to make me laugh when it was so needed. There were moments in this relationship that seemed exciting, I had someone who "wanted me", someone to text me, tell me that I was beautiful. Deep down, I knew this was not my "happily ever after" I wanted it so badly. John was not saved and did not go to church, he had a belief in God, but that is as far as it went at this time in his life. This would make us, as I knew, unequally yoked. Not to mention, it was a relationship full of ifs and maybes and when's. He was recovering from a failed marriage and was in the middle of a divorce. With a child he adopted but he still clamed as his. I respected him so much and was one of the things that drew me to him, his love for that little one. I thought God, I can help him, I can help him. I was also close to his family whom I had known from the church I was attending; I remember just dreaming about being a part of this family and really being a part of a family. As much as I loved the thought of it because I just enjoyed being around his family, they treated me as I was a part of the family his two brother's stepmother and his father. I had a great relationship with them so many great memories, I knew it was not right and it wasn't going to really happen. But I sure did fill myself with the lies saying things like, "oh he's just taking things slow because he just got out of a relationship a marriage that's big" or "he will go to church and then everything will change then". This went on for about 4 months then we had a big blow out fight and things ended.

I was alone a lot more, along with to put it plainly things started to change at my church and things where shifting. This affected me greatly, I was not as involved, things were not what they once were. All around there was a shift in my life and it felt all at once there were a lot of changes happening.

# CHAPTER 10

# PIECES OF CHANGE

*I*f I could describe my life at this time, with one word I would use transformation. In other words, "Change ". Most people don't like change I happen to hate it. Although I know in the end the change will turn out to be good. Going through the pain of change is never easy.

As Joyce Meyer says:

"You can suffer the pain of change or suffer remaining the way you are."

You may be thinking with all that you have overcome with all that you have been blessed with, why would change be so hard? Change even when it hurts is a good thing in the end, why would change make you so upset? I know all these things to be true, but I am also human like everyone else. Unfortunately, things that once gripped your heart, mind, and soul. Are the very things, if you allow them to take over they will overtake you. That is what I allowed to happen. Believing the negative thoughts when they started to creep back in. I invited depression back in, yes depression! As humans the moment we take our eyes off the Lord even for a moment, looking at our circumstances and focus on "how we Feel" and listening to our negative thinking. Doing this we are leaving the door wide open for the enemy to walk in and use things such as anger, oppression, and depression right on into our lives. You may be asking yourself, Esther, you know better, God has brought you so far how could this happen? how are you dealing with something you dealt in the beginning of your journey with God?

The very thing that gets to you will be the thing the devil will try to use against you. It's up to us to make the choice to allow those things that bring you down. For me it has been sadness and Depression. For someone else it could be drug use, drinking and drunkenness, severe anxiety or just eating too much. Anything we have ever struggled with in life, can try and come back. The best part about God, that is amazing to me, no matter how many times we fail, fall or even if we have pushed God away. God knows our every step, our every fail and mistake, we will ever make. Yet in his amazing love, He loves us through it. In the end all we have do, is call on His name and He is right there to forgive us and love us, because that is just who He is.

In James 3:2 NIV It says, "We all stumble in many ways. Anyone who is never at fault in what they say is perfect, able to keep their whole body in check."

In Jeremiah 1:5 NIV It says, "Before I formed you in the womb I knew you, before you were born, I set you apart"

There were two major changes happening. First, Spiritually, the place I have called my church home for just about 13 years of my life was changing. Things where not the same as they once were. The place that helped me drastically change my life in so many great ways, was now facing a time where things just where not the same. To say it nicely, it seemed to be falling apart. It had been happening for some time, but it was this time in my life where I needed Spiritual guidance and help. It just wasn't there as it once had been. As these thoughts and feelings of depression crept in.

Second my best friend, someone I could always count on, was now getting married. As exciting as this was to me, it was also devastating. Now that you know my story this far, you can somewhat sympathize and understand why this change for me was so hard. Because of all the old emotions, I dealt with growing up "everyone always leaves". I thought that's it she's going to leave. I also was, the last of the single friends within my group. Audra was the last single friend I had. Also, I since before I could remember I had wanted that "happy ever after". It became a party to the enemy. I began thinking and believing, things like, "you see everyone in your life leaves you",

"You will never be good enough to have anything close to what your friends have", "you are fat and lonely and that's all you will ever be", "you are nothing", "worthless" etc. As these thoughts began to fill my brain you would think well, Esther, you know what to do, but as I said I am human. I began to give in, to not just the thoughts I was thinking, but feeling the heavy feelings, that came with the thoughts. I did try to push past it, keeping a smile on my face, trying not to let everyone know what was happening inside. I learned a long time ago, what you don't deal with will eventually deal with you. I did not deal with the feelings. I didn't deal with it, God's way, I dealt with it, in my own human way. I allowed depression and all that comes with it to slowly creep back in and speak to me. At the same time, I was truly happy for my best friend. However, I felt as though I would never find the same happiness. She than asked me to be her maid of honor. I was so excited and for the next year threw myself into the planning of her big day. It was a year with waves of emotions, working long nights making hand made things for different events, smiling

while everyone was around, then crying myself to sleep at night. Me being the best friend I began to think, how dare I be upset in any way. It would be selfish to speak of my feelings and I never did. Even though I had these feelings, I truly at the same time loved her so much and wanted all these amazing things for her. My heart was breaking, thinking, and knowing that things in our relationship would change and that I would be alone again. With no one who understood me the way she had. It was such a weird time, I never experienced being happy and sad at the same time. In the end my love for her overshadowed how I felt.

I am going to be very real and say I wasn't always the best at hiding how I felt, but I did the best I could. Using the distraction of pouring everything I had left inside of me to make sure she had the best day. I just threw myself into helping and planning. Also, in this time of change, I was not dealing with what I was going through internally. I slowly started to take my eyes off God and looking to him for happiness. I was using people, things, and upcoming events like the excitement of the wedding. To fill that place in my life and I stopped looking to Him.

So, you may be asking your self does that mean you stopped loving and following God? No, I didn't, I still loved him and even knew him, but I put him in a box tucked away. I was still the honest loving Christian following Him, but I was walking around with so much undealt with hurt. I pulled Him out just on Sunday. Slowly but surely, I started to lose a grip on my life because I was not happy. I knew what to do with what I was feeling and knew I should get help. I didn't, I took the easy way fleshly way out in a sense. It was easier to give in to the depression rather than to fight against it. I also did not have the same support Spiritually, I once had and that did not make matters any better.

I wanted so bad to find my own happiness, I thought I had. I was so hopeful about this one, in the mist of this heaviness and hard time in my life. I thought yes, the light in the mist of all this darkness. He had gone to the church I was attending, I thought he was it! He had everything, a great Job, a love for the Lord and great looking, hmm, how could this end badly right? I ran into him on one of the dating sites I had been on, I was the go getter, so I reached out to him on Facebook where we were friends. After reaching out, we exchanged numbers, seemed to hit it off. Messages every morning like "Good morning beautiful" or "how's your day going," I would get from him, not to mention the long phone calls. Then there was our first date that was so magical or so I thought that lasted 8 hours. Yes, lady's I said it 8 hours! 8 hours of conversation flowing. It felt so magical that there was even the most beautiful sunset we could see through glass coffee shop we went to. I will say, I thought after that night this is it, he is the ONE.

Days passed we went on a few dates; I then began to feel him starting to pull away. This went on for about two months, it felt so amazing. I was on cloud nine! We had a double date set I was extremely, excited it was with Audra and Kenny her fiancé. Yes, for once I wasn't gonna be the third wheel. I had the whole thing planned because that's what I do right? I asked him and Audra about it and they both agreed the date was set! We talked about this for at least a week. I texted him reminding him of it, about two days before his response was "what double date?" I thought oh he's just being silly he forgot no big deal. I said "oh the one with my Audra and Kenny her fiancé. He then said, "Oh yeah that, what day was that again?" I told him the day, he said "I have a BBQ to go to that day, I'm sorry I can't go". The next morning, I opened Facebook, only to find out the man that had just told me multiple times days before that he "Missed me and couldn't wait to see me". He changed his status to say, he was in a relationship with someone else. I just remember how much these words got me right down to the core. Every word I read I cried. I remember being in complete shock. It was a Sunday. I somehow still made it to church, and I was just in a big cloudy haze. It somewhat felt as though I was living in a big haze. I wanted so much to find that thing we all want, happiness. Things had changed so much at church that counseling for me with someone I trusted had become a far distant thought. Shortly after I remember, this tremendous wave of depression. I began to feel like a heavy blanket start to cover me. The days just started to be mundane and seem the same. Day after day, I felt a piece of me fade. I was losing my will for life, thinking things would not get better. I would not ever be happy. I had seen so many of my friends build relationships and get married. Some even began to build families. Here I was stuck just me. All I ever wanted was that dream of a family filled with unconditional love. Audra was happily married, the dynamic of our relationship changed. With so many things changing and happening at once, I came to a place of hopelessness. I came to the point of feeling and wanting to give up on everything. The thoughts of suicide began to fill my every day. Then the day came when the thoughts were so strong on me that I had made the decision that I would take my life.

## CHAPTER 11

# PIECES OF UNSPEAKABLE PAIN

*I* will never forget that day, I was at the Hauk Home cleaning as I did every week. I still needed a little extra money. They were nice enough to use me even after not needing me. This day I was mopping standing in the kitchen. Karen, looked at me asked "what was wrong? Are you ok?" (Because I was always so upbeat and talkative.) That day I just listened to sad music as I cleaned crying silently) I just looked at her, she was someone I truly loved and couldn't lie to) and said no I'm not and you would be so upset if you knew my thoughts (with tears in my eyes). She then said, "you're not thinking of killing yourself, are you?" I, answered yes with tears streaming down my face she then said, "Esther no, you can't do that come on, we love you, and what about the kids and how they would feel?" I then said, "they will be ok they will be fine without me". I can't get the look of fear and sadness that filled her eyes out of my mind, from that night as I left her house. Karen knew about my past.

All that I had gone through, and even that I had dealt with sui-cide. She still loved me. She never judged, me she understood how intensely hard my life had been. That is how she knew just from the look on my face that those thoughts had been going through my head. What could she do she had never dealt with someone who had dealt with things like I had, she had no Idea what do, she wanted to stop me from leaving but I was a grown woman. What could she do? So, she let me go home with the promise I wouldn't do anything that night, that I would seek out help. She remined me all I still had, how loved I was, and that I should call seeking counseling. Reminding me that I had insur-ance, it would be paid for. I kept my promise, went home still feeling the same and cried myself to sleep.

Woke up the next morning, with the same feeling of heavi-ness and hopelessness. I did my mundane normal routine and went into the office. I went in early around 6 am. I did work as normal, took a few breaks, walked outside doing the research Karen had suggested. Doing all that I could to find a thera-pist from a list my insurance provider gave me for a therapist in my area. As the morning went on I got a call from Karen asking, "how I was and that she was glad to hear my voice" She was super encouraging telling me things would get better, I just needed to get help. After Hanging up with Karen I felt a little bit lighter full of hope that maybe she's right and things will be better. It also felt Good to know just how much she really cared for me and was there for me. I went back to work than took another break and I called at least 7-10 places that my insurance provider had given me. Each place told me that there was a two or three and in some cases four week wait for an appointment. I just remember all the hope I had begun to build with talking with Karen just began to shatter. Thanking, I just cannot take the way I am feeling one more day. I needed to get help now not in two weeks or more. I made all the phone calls I could and returned to work. With hope from one the therapist, telling me she may be able to get me in sooner. She said, she would call later in the day and let me know. The workday ended; I went straight home after. I remember this day so well; it plays like a movie in my mind as I think of it. I got home and once again broke down. I just remember screaming as I walked in the door falling to my knees weeping. I began screaming saying, I cannot do this God. I just cannot take one more day of feeling this way. I made it back to my room and I fell asleep, I was awakened by the call from the therapist, I answered the phone call from the therapist. She began to tell me how sorry she was, but she could not get me in till next week. I honestly do not remember what my response was to her I just remember the thoughts that went through my head in that moment. The thoughts were "I can't, I just can't "I got off the phone with her and began planning, a plan to end my life. It was so surreal I watched all of my TV shows I had been watching at the time, I then said, "after these shows are done that's it, I'm going to do it". Hang myself from the door of my closet in by bedroom, with a scarf. I also looked up "how long would it take for someone to die from hanging themselves". I am sure at this point your probably thinking to yourself where was my faith? why didn't I turn to God? The way for me to describe this time in my life was depression had taken hold of me so strongly I could not see any other way out. The way I describe suicide, it was like

119

emotionally my body and mind were on fire hurting so badly. I just wanted it all to stop. Just think of someone who is in fact physically burning they are so desperate for that pain and burning to stop that they would probably do just about anything. That's the place mentally I was bought to I was blinding of God's love. My mind was clouded with all things that come from the enemy. In fact, the enemy had me right where he wanted me.

John 10:10 ESV says, "The thief comes only to steal and kill and destroy.

I came that they may have life and have it abundantly."

1 Peter 5:8 AMPC says, "Be well balanced (temperate, sober of mind), be vigilant *and* cautious at all times; for that enemy of yours, the devil, roams around like a lion roaring [in fierce hunger], seeking someone to seize upon *and* devour."

These verses explain everything that was happening to me, the enemy saw and knew my every weakness. He used that old heavy weight of depression, feelings of loneliness and failure from all that I had gone through that year. I was wrong because I knew and know who I am in Christ but over time through circumstances, I allowed the enemy to come in and feed me lies and I began believing the lies.

Forming this plan of what I was going to do and how I would do it, I knew I had to drown out any hopes of living or wanting to live. So, I also decided to drink alcohol, so I went in the kitchen, made an extremely strong drink, and then headed back to my room. Just began to drink it fast while sobbing and creating a noose with a scarf. I had a song playing on loop it described how I felt. I than said I had to say goodbye to those closest to me. I sent a text message to all of them saying the same thing. "I love you and I'm sorry." After sending the text I drank most of what was left of the strong drink, stood on a stool put the noose around my neck, then kicked the stool from underneath me. Everything from this point it a bit of a blur I remember losing breath and my breath leaving me. At the same time, I remember seeing my phone blow up with phone calls as it had been from the moment, I sent out the text message. As I began losing my breath, I was holding on to the front of the noose I created and suddenly, I fell, and the noose had come apart. As I fell to the ground, I just remember weeping screaming that it had not worked. Then a rush of anger came upon me. I got up remembering in that moment that I also had some sleeping pills under my sink in the bathroom. I stumbled as I did I, was drunk. I got up went over my bathroom and began to look for the pills pulling everything out from underneath the sink. Found them and went over to my bed side all while still sobbing, distrait and shaking. Looking for a drink, I separated the pills into a pile on my bed (the pills were large) and some I had in my hand. I took the first handful of 3-4 pills and as I did, I heard a loud nock at the door. I took a few more thinking no I have got to do this. Also thinking someone I had texted called the police on me. Thinking they are just going to lock me up again, I heard the loud knock. Something inside told me to stop, I threw the pills on the floor and fell on the floor sobbing. I somehow mustered up the strength to crawl to answer the door. There is a long hallway before getting to the kitchen and Livingroom. This part hazy, but I know I eventually made it to the door fully expecting it to be the police. As I opened the door, I saw a flashlight It was one of my 2nd pastor at the time and his wife. He made a funny comment as he did most times. I remember I fell to my knees and began sobbing. His wife met me in front of the door floor, wrapped her arms around me and began to pray over me. I remember screaming "I just want to die; I just want to die I can't take this anymore". They both began praying over me. I saw and knew I heard Uncle Leos voice asking questions, being one of the ones I had sent the text message. I did not however send the text message to the pastor or his wife, but I did in fact had sent it to my best friend Madi in California and she contacted Mary who was at the church, Mary was pregnant with her first child and her husband did not want her to go to my house incase things where bad in her condition. Mary told Jen, who was one of the leaders of a youth event going on who could not leave. Jen asked the pastor and his wife to come over to check on me.

*(This part of the story to me is utterly amazing. As much as I regret that day and the choices that I made and the people I hurt. It amazes me how God was still working even when I had given up. He used my friend from California across the country to save my life. Although she was not in the same state her phone call got people to my door just in time before I had any time to make any more bad choices.*

*Although I had been so far from God at this time in my life allowing depression and oppression to take over as it very well, did God was still there and still with me even in those moments. He used the people in my life who loved me dearly to help save me.*

*(2 Tim 2:13 NASB says, If we are faithless, He remains faithful; he cannot deny himself.*

*That's what's so amazing about God he is always faithful even when we are not and don't deserve it.)*

From here on its all a big blur, I was hysterical, and drunkenness had set in. I just remember hearing multiple times "what did you take?" honestly, I do not remember the answer. I have flashes in and out of being in a car then being taken to the hospital. I do how ever remember the moment in the cloudiness realizing that I was in the hospital and though because it has happened before and by law anyone in the state of Florida who tries to harm themselves. Is kept for a mandatory psychiatric evaluation period minimum of three days or more. Me knowing this I knew I was not going home, the next thing I remember is hearing my mother enter the room then the next thing I heard was something I wish I could forget. My mother screaming a gut-wrenching cry, this I will never forget (only a mother could understand this kind of pain). She screamed say "Baby why would you do this? I love you so much" then just lots of screaming from there.

# CHAPTER 12

# PIECES OF GODS REDEEMING LOVE

*T*he next morning, I woke up in a psychiatric ward to someone screaming. I opened my eyes with instant regret in mind, as well as being scared out of my mind knowing I did not belong in this place. I remember just immediately crying. Thinking what I have done and all the people I involved and hurt. I cried asking God to forgive me for what I had done. All I wanted was out of that place. It was a cold, bare, and an unwelcoming place. It was filled with chao, people screaming, some laughing, it without reason. I was a very scary place to be for someone who was sober in other words in their right mind. As I laid there crying feeling overwhelming regret I was still hurting inside. Nothing had been fixed. Nothing had changed except being in a place I did not want to be. I began to cry louder as this realization of guilt, regret and hurt sank in, so much so a nurse came in and said "Are you ok? "I replayed sniffling, "yes, I want to go home this place is so scary". The nurse then said "I can tell you right now you're in here mandatory three days and you won't be going home any time soon. If, you don't stop crying so loudly we will come in and will sedate you. Which may result in you staying longer. So, If I where you I would stop! (With an angry, annoyed voice). So of course, I stopped out of fear of what I was told. I just for some time after just laid there silently crying my eyes out. I must have tired myself out from crying. I fell asleep waking up to a nurse asking if I wanted to eat because I hadn't eaten breakfast it was lunch time now, I answered, "No thank you". She (A nice different nurse) then said, "If you don't eat sweetie the doctor will be concerned, and you may not go home when you are supposed to you really should try eating", "I said OK, can I please have my lunch?" I then managed to get down as much as I could. Soon after finishing the nurse told me, I had a phone call. It was my mother She asked "how are you? you doing alright? Why would you do that?"

(I won't even lie with an annoyed voice; I still had been holding unforgiveness in my heart toward her) I said, "I am hurting, now is not the time to ask I want to get out of here!" She then said "come on talk to me I'm your mother I love you, you can come to me talk to me" (Unfortunately, because there was still so much in our relationship that needed to be worked on still, I just stopped years before looking for a mother's love from her because of so much that happened her being part of the reason why I was hurting I just couldn't go to her and let her in.)"I then said I'm fine I'm just hurting I regret what I did," She then put my sister on the phone, I don't remember much of that conversation to be honest. That day the calls just kept flooding in, I apologized with every phone call with mostly saying "I wanted to go home". Then Karen called, I just immediately started crying as she asked me how I was, I felt so much more guilt and hurt talking to her being that I told her how I was feeling, she said, she was so concerned, tried to get me help and did what she could to help me. She was my safe place, someone who had been there for me. Just the thought of the pain, she would have had to live with for the rest of her life. If my suicide attempt had not failed, not to mention the fact that I promised her to get help. I said, "I'm so sorry, I'm so sorry, I was just hurting, and I tried but they couldn't get me in, and I just felt I just couldn't do it one more day". She said, "It was ok, I am just happy that you're ok", then began telling me how much she loved and care for me. She than began asking me about where I was and what it was like. Right away she said, "can I come get you?" I then told her the rules of how it had to be three days. We talked for a long time. We talked about everything and nothing, anything to keep my mind busy. I told her, I wished I could just give her a big hug. She called me every day. Our conversations each time, were the same as the first, as long as possible. She wanted to be there for me as much as she could. That is what she could do so she called. While in there I got quite a few calls, so much that a woman who had also been a patient stopped me one day as I was walking to my room saying "Wow you are so loved, I have been here a few times before, I struggle with drug addiction. I have never seen anyone get as many calls as you have". We sat down and she began telling me her story. As I listened, I realized how blessed I was to have so many people call and care about me. Knowing how many times I heard "I love you" in each of the phone calls I had gotten. The day finally came the doctor called me in for a final interview. I thought yes, I'm going home! He asked a few questions one of them was "do you live alone?" I told him yes, he said, "well, you still look depressed, and I am going to make you stay longer". Signed a paper walked out I said, "I'm ok please let me go home please this place is making me depressed." He just dismissed me and told me" I'm sorry I have no choice but to leave you here". I was so upset I began crying as I walked out of the area where the interview took place went straight to the phone calling Karen, I told her, and she was so angry! She wanted to help but could not. She was not on any of my paperwork. So, two more days I stayed it was not easy or fun, but I somehow made it through. I got released uncle Leo and Aunt Mary Lou took me home. After praying with me I thanked them, they left, I took a much-needed shower. The simple things you miss. I then packed a few things and headed over to Karen's, I had not seen her in over a week. I knew staying at home was not the best, I needed to be around people who loved me. I walked into Karen's and the one thing I had asked for almost, now a week ago, she gave me right in that moment as I walked into the room, she threw her arms open and embraced me. I emphasize this for two reasons one big reason is the fact that this is not Karen's personality, she is not a mushy hugger at all. Also, because to the attention to detail she remembered what I said I needed a week prior, and boy, did I need it. Earl and the kids were not home it was just the two of us, we sat and talked for a while. Earl and the Kids came home, the kids asked why I was staying there but were not told why I was there. Only that I was sad and needed not to be alone. They didn't care they were excited for me to be around more. The love these kids had for me and still have for me means so much. I just remember in those first moments of them coming home in the back of my mind thinking how sad they would have been. I hugged them a little tighter. Tyler was 12 and Madison was 9, I did not want them to know. I remember Earl was super sweet too, I was so blessed I know I was right where I needed to be. Now that I was in a good healthy safe environment with all the love and support, I needed. It was time to heal and get the help I needed most importantly I first repented that night I got down on the floor of the room and asked God to forgive me for what I had tried to do. Almost every morning I would start my day with Joyce Meyer her real and raw preaching had always helped me. I still attended the church I was going to on Sundays. I also started a search eventually finding a good christen counselor I was on the road to healing. Things started to look up after about a month or so I went home again, I was I felt it was time. I was told I could stay as long, as I needed, I wasn't rushed out in the least in the time of me staying there the whole family and I had gotten a whole lot closer. This was for me the time where I really began to look to Karen as like a mother. Although it truly isn't part of her personality to be soft and nurturing, not that she can't be that way, but each person has their way of doing things. She had always been a nice caring person. Also, very tough yet sweet and logical person. She saw and knew what I needed and tapped more into that nurturing side of herself for sure and I would say she defiantly pulled out all the stops for me. She did all that she could do to help me. I believe whole heartedly, God allowed this to happen. In a time when I needed it most. Karen told me how she thought I was doing so well when I was going to church more often that she thought I should get back to going regularly. God used her to lead me back to him. She would also remind to listen to Joyce Meyer. She knew how much it helped mentally and spirituality. Her Knowing when these things were aligned in my life that mentally I was at a good place with Gods help. As time went on and our relationship grew, I can't say I was always the easiest person to deal with. But through it all she has stood by me and told me she would never walk away. I have to say, for me this was so big, to hear, being that so many have walked away. Understandably in some circumstances, dealing with someone who is so broken and hurt emotionally is not easy to deal with and even love. She has with many others have shown me what unconditional love, and what that looks and feels like. I continued to go the christen counselor now you may be thinking why I keep saying "christen counselor" and not just "counselor", I say that because I believe this kind of counselor made all the difference, she put God in the center of all her counseling and I believe that makes a huge difference. She was not just helping me mentally but also spirituality. Within a year I was at such a better place, I continued to do all the things I needed to become healthier mentally and spiritually. We prayed at the start and end of each session. She often would refer to what God's word said on each thing we spoke about it. It helped me build a strong relationship with him again. After a year, I then started to add getting healthy. I have always been an emotional eater, eating unhealthy things to get by. I began learning about eating healthy with Karen's help and how much it would be help me mentally to start eating heathy. I also started a great journey, into working out. I started working out with Karen going to this amazing, sweet, and uplifting encouraging trainer Drew. He was just another vital part of my healthy journey he was super up lifting and when I would fail or felt that I could not, he reminded me how it was possible! I then came to one of the heathiest happiest places of my life. During these two years of getting myself better Spiritually and mentally, I still tried talking with my family mostly my mother because no matter how hard things where she was my mother and I still loved her. I also knew what God's word says about forgiveness. I tried so, so hard, at times and because of anger (I wasn't perfect) I would also reject her but the one thing I never stopped doing was trying. With God's help and guidance So there were still good times with her.

# CHAPTER 13

# PIECES OF CONSUMING CANCER

*A*s you all know from my story, my mother was diagnosed with cancer when I was fifteen. Just as I was getting to this great and healthy place, I got the news that my mother's cancer had come back with a vengeance. This time it completely began to take over as she grew weaker and frail. She went from a person who seemed very healthy and lively in one year went downhill very fast. It began with the frequent visits to the hospital. I was getting physically and mentally in a great place I was working out regularly. I had also decided to work as a fulltime nanny. I had a great challenging but fulfilling job, working with three amazing children who I loved and still love so much! They brought so much joy to my life in a time where it just got so hard and even unbearable. It seemed they just kept me going, keeping a smile on my face even on my worse of days. That year my mom had been in and out of the hospital at least 100 or more times. The cancer began to take over, her breathing and immune system was just about gone. She began constantly calling me asking for help. At first this was a struggle because of where our relationship. As well as she was not always the kindest sick person. I could see how bad it was getting. My sister also at times stepped into help until it became too overwhelming. So I had a decision to make, to help my mother who I knew and could see was clearly dying or go on with my life and hope she gets better and do the bare minimum what did I do? , I had to step in and help of course no matter what as I said she was my mother I love her so much It killed me inside to see she was now dying. I began going over to her apartment after work. I would work caring for three children and at night go over and help her. I made sure she ate, had meds and even at times massage her due to so much pain. She would almost be in tears. It was like watching a flower slowly wither. She was never extremely healthy when she had cancer. This time I just knew it was the worse then I had ever seen. I was praying one day, and I felt God tell me her time was running short. How long was that a day? A week or a year? That I did not know, I just knew it was not long. My sister and brother would stop and help when they could. It wasn't enough She needed so much more help. I made the decision to give everything up to help her. My life would now consist of work and work caring for her. I began going over after work to help. My job also allowed me to take the little boy I was caring for with me during the day. Sometimes, to check in on her at home or even times when she was admitted in the hospital. He really lit her up, she just loved him! I would do all I could to help her. Being completely honest, it was so, overwhelming I wanted to run away once again. I just felt hopeless watching her die. It began to get overwhelming going to work and then leaving to care for her. Then she had gotten a bit stronger for about a week and things seemed to be looking up. So, I took a break. A break for myself one weekend spending time with friends trying to escape the reality of what was happening. I would call her and check on her making sure she was ok. That weekend on Sunday I was with my friend Kristy who was looking at new houses. I couldn't get a hold of her; I began to panic thinking something was wrong. Her apartment was not far from where I lived but it was not convenient to get to her if I had needed to get to her fast. Then when she did respond I had been even farther away about thirty minutes away. I didn't have my car at the time ether. I had my friend drop everything quickly taking me back to my car. I got into my car, and I began to panic even more. I finally got to her. She was in extreme amount of pain, was throwing up, and had trouble breathing. I nearly carried her to the car, and I quickly rushed her to a hospital close to her in Tampa. The hospital did all the normal things like taking her, vitals and started medications. The doctor came in and said "there was not much we can do for her. She is dying, and she just needed to get comfortable". I was angered by this as I wasn't ready to let her go. I knew she had some fight left in her. I think this hospital was just understaffed and was tired of seeing her as she had been back to that hospital so many times that year, I would say even that week. That they were just done seeing her. I told her after that day I would not take her back there anymore. If she had to go to the hospital, I would take her to the one by my house which I happen to think was better anyway. After that happened, I told her it was a lot going back and forth as I had been doing this for a few months. I asked, her if she would move in with me. I was going to continue to care for her, she said yes. So, we planned it out that she would move in within the month. I slowly moved all her things in, she was now living with me. Let's just say now that I was more involved, I began to see the reality of what the doctors and nurses tried to tell me at the other hospital. They just weren't very nice by the way they said it. I began to see how bad she was not eating. Day by day since she moved in, I began to see her fading. Not to mention she demanded much more of my attention, and I still had a full-time job. I knew that I had her get her affairs in order paying for her funeral. It became overwhelming, it got worse when she moved in because now, she was even more reliant on me than before. In getting advice on what to do for help I found out how to get Hospice Care involved. I asked Karen, to help me speak to my mother, to help her understand how much they could help. Their services where not just for people who were dying but also for those who were clinically ill. The fact she did not have the best memory, some days she did not always take her meds. I'm not a nurse to help with that, Hospice helped. I could call them any time she needed something, and they could come to help. This was perfect, or so I thought. She was a fighter always fisty, very prideful and wasn't happy about this situation, I now know too that it truly was also fear. She wasn't ready to die, she was only 57 years old. Any person that hears Hospice thinks about death. A lot of people don't know all the ins and outs of all their services. I knew nothing, until I was told and learned it, I thought the same thing. I knew time was coming soon by seeing her condition, but I did not know when. I wanted and needed two things at this time to happen. One, to help prolong and preserve her life, long as I could doing everything possible. I also needed some of this pressure to be taken off me. Mainly during the day when I had to work. I feared I would end up losing my job. That would not have helped ether of us. With hospices help I saw the light at the end of this tunnel. Hospice not only could take the pressure off me, but they would take the best care of her when I could not be there. Her immune system being so weak, it was best that she did not go in and out of the hospital every time she felt sick or pain. It would not have been a good choice for her to do that, so it was best for Hospice to come in and take care of her. But for her this meant she was dying, and she did not like it at all. She didn't like the idea; she wasn't on board with it. She would say things like, "I don't need Hospice, I'm not dying". I then told her how much it would help me help her. She agreed to it for me because she knew I was trying to help her. She fought it just about every step of the way and it made life still extremely hard. Hospice was the logical decision. They would come to our home and help her with everything she needed. She would not be exposed to sicknesses or diseases in a hospital. This would help her live as long as possible. My mother didn't see it this way, it caused a lot of arguments and caused her to be very angry with me, almost all the time. My mother was and always had been outside a very independent person. On her strong days she decided that she wanted to do whatever she felt she needed to do. So, she would want to drive. I found out, that she had been given morphine for her pain. Which meant even when she was feeling well, she shouldn't be driving under the influence of that medication. She was told, she wasn't supposed to drive but she still wanted to drive. Because I had to take over becoming her caregiver if something were to happen, I would have been responsible had she had gotten into an accident. I came up with a plan to hide her car so that she would not be able to drive it. I got a letter from her doctor stating she could no longer drive because of the medication. This did not go over well. It caused one of the biggest arguments that I had ever had with my mom, since I have been an adult. She completely lost it, she called the police stating I stole her car; the police understood my side of it saying that they had dealt with this when family members have their cars taken for medical or other reasons. Because she had given me power of attorney over her, she couldn't do anything. This was like putting fuel on a fire, any spunk she had left inside she used it. That night she said, things to me that I would never want to repeat, things that no mother ever should say to their daughter. It was so hurtful and so painful; I can't even express to you the pain that I felt hearing those words come out of her mouth. She was only at my house for about a month when this all happened. It had gotten so bad after she called the police on me thinking that she can get her car back. Got my sister involved because my sister's name was on her car. It was just a huge mess. She still had her apartment because it was still paid up for a few months. I was going to use the extra time to go over and clean it for her since she moved out. She was so upset, she wanted to move out right away. As fragile and as sick as she was, it didn't matter there was always this strength about her that I will never under-stand and never forget. The next day, she was gone. I said to myself after this argument, I would never talk to her again I would never be able to get over what she'd said to me. How dare she say those things to me. I think at one time or another all of us in our lives have something like this about someone when they have said or done something that's very hurtful. But the difference is when God is in your life, and you love Him there is no way around unforgiveness. He will always nudge you and remind you why you should forgive. Because of what his word says, but also how it holds you in a place where you don't want to be. I didn't want to be angry at my mom, but I was. I didn't want to be so hurt inside but Even with my hard childhood and with so many undealt with issues. I tried to put all the hurt aside and I did what I could to help her. At the time I couldn't see her side of why, to be honest in a away wrote her off. I wrote her a letter and I said that I didn't want to have anything to do with helping her. I knew I couldn't tell her face to face; it was just too hard. I just gave up. I was driving up to see one of my best friends that lives in Jacksonville. Ashli and her family just to get away. I hadn't gotten away in so long and I really missed them. Talking to Cindy on the phone and telling her about the letter saying, "I'm never talking to her again, feeling that anger and feeling all of those emotions. I remember just being so infuriated that I had given up everything, everything to help her my whole life. To just get it smacked right in my face like I had done nothing, and I was the evil person it was probably one of the hardest things I've ever had to go through. Cindy said "Esther you can't do that, you're not gonna feel right if you don't talk to your mom again. I know deep down as upset as you are you still love her". Of course, I did but I was just so hurt I couldn't see past the pain I felt. Our relationship had already been rocky before I had started seriously helping her and I put all of that aside to help her. There were so many unspoken hurts I just put aside and pushed under the rug and pretended wasn't there just so that I could help her, and it still wasn't enough. For a few weeks I didn't speak to her. One day found out, that she had moved in with my uncle from my sister. I still cared even then because I would call and ask my sister how she was. I was so torn inside because I knew my mother was dying. I had given a whole year of my life to try and help take care of her. In some ways as hard as it was, I felt like a failure because I couldn't help her. I wasn't good enough. Eventually she called me and at first, I was very bitter, during this whole time of being bitter and angry, God tried to speak to me. I ignored the voice I was so angry. I truly let anger and hurt take over, But God never gives up. In my spirit He slowly but surely, He would nudge me and remind me and bring to my memory just different circumstances and reasons why I should love her.

The truth of the matter is she was dying, that scared her because of the fear she turned into a different person. The fear took over she went into a place of denial. The truth was too hard for her to digest. The things she did and said weren't right, it took some time for sure but of course I had to be there for her. At first, I kind of just had a casual conversation with her. I would keep it to normal things and not talk about health and that kind of thing. Then one day she called me crying, saying she needed to go to the hospital and there was no one there to take her. Prior to this I struggled so much spiritually and mentally with the fact that my mother was dying.

I had so much bitterness and anger that I didn't know how or what to do to let it go. Once again, she called, and I dropped everything, took her to the hospital and they did all they could to help her. They told her that she should probably get Hospice back involved but of course she didn't want to. At the time she told them that she knew all about Hospice and she didn't want to have anything to do with it. It was now almost three months after her moving out of my house, I was back to visiting her most days after work. If I was not visiting her, I was at least calling her on the phone. I started helping my uncle and sister who had been helping her. Understand what to do and how to help her. Because in the months that I had helped her I had learned so much. I do not think my uncle realized when taking her in how much care she truly needed. Slowly but surely, I got more and more involved once again. She was my mother; how could I not help that's all that I kept thinking. Then one night I went before God, and I just got on my knees, and I cried and said, "God I need to let all the pain, all of the hurt, that I feel inside go". My mother apologized for all that had happened. That helped but it wasn't enough, I was still hurt but I was still helping her too. After getting on my knees and going before God, I started to see her differently. There was a love in my heart that grew. I can't even explain, not to mention she began to change too. We were laughing more; she was giving me advice and I was taking it. I got the closest to her than I had ever in my entire life. I couldn't have been more thankful she started to become and became the mother I always wanted and needed my whole life. That was such a struggle for me because I could not understand, I would ask God all the time God why now why couldn't, I have gotten this years ago. You would think other people may think the same way but look at it in this way, I could have not understood it. I learned to be thankful for the moments that I had with her. The difference is I now began not wanting to imagine life without her. I now wanted her to be a part of my life, I now wanted her to see me get married and her to see my children. I knew deep down inside that would never happen. That broke me, I just held on to what I had. Every moment that I had left I cherished with her. At this point that's all I could do I had done all that I could to help her. I prepared for her when she did go. I had tried to help her in many other ways and only time would tell. God would know when it was her time. The waiting was probably one of the hardest parts about all of this, the waiting and not knowing, living everyday wondering when I would get a phone call and when that phone call would come. I didn't know how or when it happen. Living in so much uncertainty was not easy or fun but looking back at it I would not trade any moment that I had with her. Then one day I got a phone call at work saying that my mom was in the hospital and that I needed to get there immediately. My heart sank, I can't even explain it. I thought this is it, guilt, pain, anger, every kind of emotion you can think of hit me all at one time. I didn't want my mother to die. For once in my life, the anger that I felt didn't matter but her being around mattered more than anything else. But now it was out of my control, I got to the hospital. The doctor said, "I don't know why you keep coming back to the hospital we've done all the tests that we could possibly do". She was worse than she had ever been before, you could tell her face that she was tired she was so tired of fighting. I'll never forget everybody was gone she was laying in the bed so frail and weak. I held on to her hand and I put my head down. On this side of the bed and I just cried I cried my eyes out for the first time in my life, I felt so helpless for her more than I ever had felt before this point. I did not want her to leave, and I couldn't stop it and death became real. As I sat there crying, she looked at me and said as strong as ever and as comical ever was and said, "what are you crying for I'm not going nowhere" knowing it was her time, but she just had to say something to be strong for me. That was her way of trying to stop me from hurting. You may be asking yourself how, how this could be possible. The only way I could explain it is the redemption and love of Jesus. He brought restoration to our relationship, there is no other rhyme or reason that I could ever express. There was restoration so much that it was so much more painful to let her go. My heart aches for her in a different way it never had before. When she was sick the anger inside, I felt wasn't anger at her, it was anger for wanting her to live longer. It was so hard to come to terms with this, but I knew her time was very, very short at this point. Little did I know doctors said within a few days it would happen. Inside I was so angry and was filled would so much confusion and hurt because how could God fix it and then take it away? I could not understand. In that moment of anger and sadness I felt as if God whispered to me, changing my prospective, in that moment I also realize he did not give it and take it away. But that he had yet allowed her to live just long enough so that he could mend our relationship that had been broken for so long. In fact, He had given me just what I always wanted and needed my entire life. I began to see the blessing in it, I was no longer angry yet sad and grateful.

With what was to come in the next few days, I would really need his help. How God? How will I get through letting her go?

# AUTHOR'S MESSAGE

My hope is after sharing my story with you. If there is anything in your life you may be struggling with. You know who you can turn to find healing, hope and restoration Jesus can do all that He has done for me for you! He has taken all my broken pieces and made them into something beautiful. No matter where you are or what your story is He can and will change your life if you let him. He's just waiting for you to ask, and let Him in. God love us all as his children but gives us the choice to choose him. Trust me choose Him, there is no better way. You will never experience more unconditional love by making this one choice in your life, to choose him.

# APPENDIX

# SALVATION IS FREE

"For God so loved the world that he gave his one and only Son, that whoever believes in him shall not perish but have eternal life." John 3:16 NIV

"And everyone who calls on the name of the Lord will be saved" Acts 2:21 NIV

Who is the leader of your life? In Romans 10:9-10 NKJV, says that if you confess with your mouth the Lord Jesus and believe in your heart that God raised Him from the dead, you will be saved. For with the heart one believes unto righteousness, and with the mouth confession is made unto salvation.

It says that if we declare that Jesus is Lord, we will be saved. If you are ready to go all in and follow Jesus pray this prayer.

"Jesus, thank you for dying on the cross for my sin, and rising from the dead to give me new life. I repent of my sin and turn to you. Today I choose to follow you with all my heart for the rest of my life. I believe in you and declare you to be the leader and Lord of my life. Thank you for forgiving me and walking with me from this moment forward! Amen.

Salvation Prayer written by Ruben Cruz<br>Lead Pastor of Refuge Church

*Worshiping with music, has been a large part of my healing journey. Here is a list of songs that have helped me, songs that have spoken to me throughout the years. During these times of worship, I would just cry out to God, His presence would just fill the room. I believe these songs can do the same for you.*

- Wrap Me in your arms by Michael Gungor
- It is well by Bethel Music
- Be still by Bethel Music
- I can feel you by Bethel Music
- I love your presence by Bethel Music and Jenn Johnson
- Healer by Bethel Music, Leah Mari
- Loved me by JJ heller
- In the morning by JJ Heller
- Oceans by Hillsong Worship
- What a Beautiful Name by Hillsong Worship
- Steady My Heart by Kari Jobe
- Revelation song by Kari Jobe
- I am not Alone by Kari Jobe
- Be still My soul by Kari Jobe
- Oh how He Loves by David Crowder Band

- Reason to sing by All sons & Daughters
- How can it be by Lauren Daigle
-You Say by Lauren Daigle
-Take Me to the King by Tamela Mann
- Letting go by Steffany Gretzinger
- Good Good Father by 10,000 fathers, Georgie Wilkins
- I will follow you by Forerunner Music, Misty Edwards
- Clean by Nataile Grant
- King Of the world by Nataile Grant
- Held by Nataile Grant
- My Weapon by Natalie Grant
- Face to Face by Nataile Grant
- Burn Bright by Nataile Grant
- Let it Happen by United Pursuit, Andrea Mari
- My world needs you by Kirk Franklin, Sarah Reeves, Tasha Cobbs
- Lay It All Down by Will Regan, United Pursuit
- The Blessing by Kari Jobe and Cody Carnes
- Nothing Else by Cody Carnes
- Promises by maverick city music
- Refiner by maverick city music
- Voice of God by Dante Bowe,Stephanie Gretzinger and Chandler Moore

CPSIA information can be obtained
at www.ICGtesting.com
Printed in the USA
LVHW051949060921
697132LV00005B/130